THE
LIVING
COMMANDMENTS

John Shelby Spong

A CROSSROAD BOOK
THE SEABURY PRESS
NEW YORK

1977 · *The Seabury Press*
815 Second Avenue · New York, N.Y. 10017

Library of Congress Cataloging in Publication Data

Spong, John Shelby.
The living commandments.
"A Crossroad book."
1. Commandments, Ten—Addresses, essays, lectures.   I. Title.
BV4655.S66   241.5′2   77–8344
ISBN 0–8164–0356–2

For my parents, Doolie Griffith Spong (1907–   )
and John Shelby Spong (1889–1943),
who taught me my first lessons in life and who
provided me with the capacity to love,
the security to live and the courage to be.

Contents

Preface

This book was born at St. Paul's Church, Richmond, Virginia, in a lecture series given on Sunday mornings. In my experience of twenty-two years in the ministry, I have never known a congregation so vibrant, so alive, so eager to search and explore the frontiers of contemporary life from the vantage point of a deep and significant Christian commitment. These lectures were also broadcast over WRFK–FM in Richmond and resulted in much public discussion. The response encouraged me to seek publication.

Every author knows that between lectures and a published volume there is a great gulf, fixed, and for me that gulf included a transition from being rector of St. Paul's to being a bishop in the Diocese of Newark. I have always written in a community of critics, advisors, and editors. That community was in Richmond, and yet the final writing of this book took place in Newark, so it was a far more arduous and lonely task than I had imagined. But it has been done, and in some sense my worlds have been combined in this effort.

My thanks for helpful assistance go to so many:

To Lucy Newton Boswell Negus, my administrative assistant in Richmond, whose editorial genius and creative abilities far surpass mine and whose constant and personal encouragement enabled me to begin a writing career in the first place.

To George Edward Rath, my senior bishop, whose pastoral sensitivity is rare among men, enabling him to discern my tensions between being an author and being a bishop, and who made it possible for me to combine the two.

To Carter Donnan McDowell, whose assistance in the rewriting of both the personal prologue and several chapters was immense.

To Dr. Robert O. Kevin, retired professor of Old Testament at the Virginia Theological Seminary, who read the material for accuracy of fact, but who, despite being my great teacher, cannot be held accountable for the accuracy or inaccuracy of interpretation.

To Eleanor Freed Evans, M.D., professor of medicine at the Medical College of Virginia, who worked particularly with me on questions that related to medical facts.

To Dr. Frank Eakin, professor of Old Testament at the University of Richmond, who was an invaluable aid in both general and specific areas.

To Cyane Hoare Lowden, who did the primary work of copy editing.

To Jo Anne Stoddard Palmore, who, despite assurance to the contrary, regards me as a hopeless conservative ethicist, and who has challenged my thinking time after time.

To Beverly J. L. Anderson, my administrative aide in Newark, whose typing, helpful suggestions, and calm personality under the stress of great provocation were deeply appreciated.

To the Rev. Martha Blacklock, Archdeacon of the Diocese of Newark and editor of the *Newark Churchman,* who saved me from many sexist prejudices.

To the Vestry of St. Paul's Church, Richmond, Virginia, and the clergy and lay people of the Diocese of Newark, for allowing me the time to prepare this manuscript.

To Robert Morgan Gilday, my editor at The Seabury Press, whose genius as an editor is exceeded only by the charm of his person and the endurance of his friendship.

And finally to my family—Joan, my wife, Ellen, Katharine, and Jaquelin, my daughters, and even to our cat, Hermann, all of whom have shared that wondrous thing called life with me so deeply and for so long, and who have blessed me time and again with love that is as undeserved as it is appreciated. To them I would say my deepest thanks, for to them I owe my deepest debt.

J. S. S.

Newark, New Jersey
January 1, 1977

The Living Commandments

1

A Personal Prologue

This is a book about ethics and rules, life and faith. It is written by one who wants to explore each of these categories.

I am not a universal man. I am a particular man with a particular heritage and particular attitudes. I have been shaped by my environment and by my century. I speak with no wisdom beyond the experiences of my life as they have interacted with my upbringing, my education, and my deepest commitments.

I am a Christian. I am convinced that in Jesus of Nazareth God has entered human history uniquely and decisively, but I am not wedded to any particular explanation as to how that great and mighty wonder actually came to pass. Above all else, I want to be an honest man. I want to be honest about what I believe and how I live that belief out, but I also want to be open and capable of moving into new conclusions should the living of life seem to push me in new directions.

I am a child of the South. My family upbringing was strict, moralistic, Calvinist. Ethical issues were not discussed in my childhood home, life's answers were considered to be clear and self-evident, leaving little room for discussion, much less for debate. Only the two categories of right and wrong seemed to exist. The content of those two categories was assumed to be certain. In that environment, to violate the rules of life was to bring swift and certain punishment upon yourself. If your bad behavior managed to escape human notice, you were assured that nothing was hidden from God's all-seeing eye. If the scales of reward and punishment for good and bad behavior were not balanced here on earth, they would be balanced—the preachers would tell you—beyond the grave in the heavenly places or in the fiery pits of hell. In my youth to be caught in wrongdoing was to experience both the fear of God and the fear of my mother! She was not a big woman, but armed with a stinging switch picked from a forsythia bush, she seemed ten feet tall to me. There was never much doubt that good and evil were clear, simple, and distinct categories.

There was tremendous security in such an upbringing. But while I enjoyed that security, I am also now aware that it produced in me an unthinking rigidity and a highly judgmental attitude, for both were distinct parts of my personality structure as a teenager. If I felt insecure or uncertain in those years, I would never have admitted it. My tendency was to cover that insecurity with dogmatic pronouncements; and this tended to make my rigidity seem virtuous, at least to myself. It is easy to understand why I was not particularly popular with my peers at that stage of my life.

By the time I was twenty-one, I had never tasted alcohol, I had finished college, I was married, and I had decided on the priesthood as my vocation and career. I suppose I saw in the priesthood an external rigidity that ministered to my needs for certainty. Yet that vocation has, much to my surprise and joy, done exactly the opposite thing for me. It has called me to live in and to appreciate the joy of uncertainty, the absence of security, and it has led me into an existential search for integrity of character and faith in a world that seems to many to have only questions and no final answers.

This is a brief description of the person who has undertaken to write this volume. I feel it essential that my reader have some sense of who I am and the direction from which I am coming, for the subject matter of this book is both personal and nonobjective.

There is still deep in my makeup that strain of moralistic rigidity. It is best expressed, I suppose, in the personal standard of conduct I impose upon myself. A sense of an ultimate right and an ultimate wrong is still real for me, and I often wonder how I would deal with any serious breach of that standard in my personal life. But this rigidity is coupled with intense and significant learning from the psychoanalytic disciplines, including a two-year seminary experience in group therapy with four other seminary couples. Beyond that, I have spent over twenty years as a pastor privileged to share in the deepest secrets and internal traumas of very real human beings. I cannot even imagine an aspect of human behavior that I have not confronted as a counselor. As a result of these experiences, I have been driven to nonmoralistic conclusions time after time. The exigencies of existence have given birth to what has become the deepest tenet of my belief, namely, that God's will for every life includes wholeness, freedom, being. The traditional moral code generally undergirds wholeness, freedom, and being, but not always, and when it doesn't, the quest for wholeness has come to take priority for me over the rules of behavior, at least as I deal with the lives of other people.

It is from this mixture of personal rigidity and pastoral openness that I entered this study of the Book of Exodus in general and the Ten Commandments in particular. I wanted to affirm the eternal truth that lies underneath this ancient code—a truth that has endured the test of time, but I also wanted to free that eternal truth from its rigid, ancient context so that it might be heard anew in the context of my world and my century. I wanted to perceive the heart of the law as the creator of wholeness rather than as the moralistic arbiter of goodness.

A book to me is a very personal thing, a sharing if you will, of what is real in the life of the author. I trust that this work will be received as such, and if some part of what is real to me makes contact with something that is real in the lives of my readers, then my purpose will have been achieved.

Shalom.

2

The Covenant and the Context— A Call in Awe and Wonder

T he Ten Commandments did not drop from heaven fully written. They did not interrupt, they rather grew out of the common life of the people of Israel. In this opening chapter we seek to create the original written context. Exodus Nineteen describes that context, portraying it as a mysterious, mystical experience of God. It is a chapter that defies rationality. Only when we enter this chapter can we properly approach what the Hebrew people called the "Ten Words" and what Christians have come to call the "Ten Commandments."

Both the early cultic use of the Ten Commandments and their present-day meaning will be sought in this volume. In this process many of the great ethical questions of this age can be confronted. In addition to that confrontation there will come the discovery that the Ten Commandments, literally understood, do not always apply. Some readers may be anxious about that. They need not be. For the moment anything is literalized, it is doomed to extinction. Only the eternal truth behind the literal word will ever endure the test of time. For example, can one really talk about the Commandment "You shall do no murder" and not raise such issues as war, capital punishment, euthanasia, or abortion? And in each of these discussions the literal position has to be compromised. That is only one of the Commandments, and it is not the most controversial Commandment of all. To enter the meaning of the Commandments, it is essential that we become less academic and more existential. On many of the contemporary, moral issues formal expertise does not dictate rightness or wrongness, for everyone has opinions and convictions and subjective attitudes, involvement, and fears. I do not write as an expert or from some ex cathedra position as if I possessed the final truth. I do write to share the gropings of my life in the field of ethics as I seek to be true to the integrity of the Christian revelation and to the integrity of the twentieth century.

In Israel's sacred history before the law which begins with the Ten Words is given, an unusual and mysterious episode described in Exodus Nineteen is recounted. This chapter is filled with interpretive problems. It is obviously a collage of more than one tradition. To separate these traditions, however, and to get back to whatever the original was, is almost as difficult as trying to reconstruct a pig from a piece of sausage. To enter Chapter Nineteen is to enter a world of images, intimate details, and mysterious words. For the children of Israel this is a momentous event in the history of nation-building. Here the Covenant is born and the national vocation as the people of God is established.

In the present text of this narrative, Moses goes up and down Mount Sinai no less than three times, and for a man reputed in the biblical tradition to be in his eighties, that is no small chore. So first we attempt to enter and understand the story as the Book of Exodus relates it, at the stage when it achieved a written form.

It is the "third moon," says the Exodus account, some ninety days after the deliverance from Egypt. This wandering Semitic band has entered the wilderness of Sinai, where they have set up their camp in front of the mountain which is forever after to be a part of their life and of their tradition. Intuitively, they seem to know that God and that mountain are connected; perhaps they even assume in a primitive way that God dwells on that mountain. Moses leaves the people, journeying up the mountain to commune with God, whereupon God directs him to speak to the Israelites. God's message is "You have seen what I did to the Egyptians. I bore you on eagle wings, and I brought you to myself. Hearken to my voice. Keep my Covenant. You shall be my people, my special possession, a kingdom of priests, a holy nation" (Exodus 19:3–6). Moses takes those words returning down the mountain. He summons the elders of the people, telling them all of the Lord's words. The people respond, "All that Yahweh has spoken, we will do."

As yet, there is no specific content. That is, no one has yet said concretely just what the mark of the Covenant people is. No one has yet asked, How does a holy nation of priests *live*? Everything is vague, and there appears to be a certain comfort in keeping it that way. It is like a group of people being told that they are to love everyone. They respond to that generalization, "Of course we will! There is no one we hate. We can easily say that we love everyone." They live happily with that resolution until they discover that when love asks "Who is my neighbor?" the answer is "Everyone," including those people regarded as social, physical, or mental inferiors. Then people say strange things reaching the absurdity of a layman who once told me: "The Commandment to go love everybody is part of a communist plot to integrate my private club or to effect open housing."

Platitudes are easy. We are comfortable with platitudes. Moses, in his first encounter with God on the mountain, comes down with nothing but a platitude: "You are to be a holy people." And Israel responds: "Lord, we will do it." Israel is still in the platitudinous stage of the Covenant: "All that the Lord has spoken, we will do."

Moses goes up the mountain again reporting this reply to God. This is an interesting image of God. He appears not to know everything that is going on. Moses must run back and forth just to keep God informed. But let us not get lost in literal details until we embrace the feeling of the drama that is unfolding before us.

God responds by saying, "Moses, I will come to you in a thick cloud in public view, so that the people may hear when I speak with you, so that they will trust you forever. You return and tell the people to prepare for that happening. Prepare today and tomorrow; be ready on the third day, for on that day God will appear on Mount Sinai. This is how you are to prepare: Wash your clothes. Set boundaries for the people;

forbid them to touch this holy mountain." Refrain from sex—
"Don't go near a woman" is the way the command is given—
making us aware that this context is clearly a patriarchal,
rather sexually chauvinistic world (Exodus 9:10–13).

It was not that these things were bad; there is no such thing
as Hebrew puritanism. Yet what was about to transpire in the
life of this nation was deemed to be so different and so life-
changing that the normal processes of life could and must be
suspended so that there might be total concentration upon this
holy event.

The third day came. When that day arrived, there were
peals of thunder and flashes of lightning. A dense cloud hov-
ered upon the mountain. There was a long blast on the cere-
monial horn, the *shofar*. It reached a relentless and ear-splitting crescendo, and Moses began to lead the people to the foot
of Mount Sinai. Then Sinai was enveloped in smoke. The
Lord was seen to come down in fire. The mountain trembled,
Moses spoke, and God answered, inviting Moses alone up into
the mountain. Moses entered that cloud and smoke. The people stood in wonder.

In that meeting, God ordered Moses one more time to warn
the people that they were not to come nearer, that they were
not to touch that holy mountain lest they die. Not even the
priests, who were considered holy people, could approach that
mountain unless they had gone through a special service of
sanctification.

Moses argued with God, saying, "Lord, you have already
commanded them not to come near the mountain. They are
going to obey." Yet God ordered him to go back down and
repeat that warning. Then he was to return with Aaron.
Moses obeyed.

The people, seeing these wonders, far from approaching the
holy place were falling back in fear. They said to Moses,
"Speak to us, and we will obey, but do not let God speak to
us, lest we die."

"Do not be afraid," Moses replied. "God has come to test
you, so that the fear of God may keep you from sinning." The
people stood at a distance, and Moses once more climbed the
mountain and entered the thick cloud where God was. When

Moses reappeared the third time, he would read to them the laws of God.

This is the setting. This is the context in which Israel's sacred history asserts that the Ten Commandments are given. It is a context that most of us are not aware of, and, consequently, we have never placed the Ten Commandments in their proper setting with the proper sense of power. Once that setting is seen, the task of probing, exploring, searching begins.

First, we look at the sources behind this episode for some insights. Scholars have identified at least four documents that lie beneath our finished Old Testament. They have named these narrative strands the Yahwist document, the Elohist document, the Deuteronomic document, and the Priestly document. In terms of each document's writing, the range in age is from the tenth century B.C. for the oldest to the fourth century B.C. for the youngest. Behind the written documents is both an ancient, oral tradition and some very particular historical circumstances and cultural phenomena which have clearly shaped the narratives. Yet even admitting all this, I suspect that there is no part of the Old Testament about which scholars are in less agreement than this present passage, for none of the ordinary rules by which the scholars separate the Yahwist document, the Elohist document, and the Priestly document, for example, seem to pertain to this passage. Nothing helps in separating the various strands of data here, yet there is no Old Testament scholar I know of who believes that the present text as our bibles have it in Exodus Nineteen is from a single source. Most of the scholars wind up saying that it is a blend of the Yahwist and Elohist documents with some editorial comments from other sources, and that the Elohist seems to prevail in certain places. Certainly we know that the Elohist document's version of the Ten Commandments is found in Exodus Twenty. The Yahwist version of the Ten Commandments is very different, rather strange and far more cultic (Exodus 34).

Most scholars think that chapters 19 and 20 are a blended text, with the Yahwist and Elohist documents being the prevailing sources. However, merger seems to have taken place while both the Yahwist and Elohist documents were in their oral tradition, which perhaps constitutes the heart of the scholar's difficult textual problem.

Inside the narrative, scholars can identify two forms, two ritual ceremonies, that seem to dominate the shape of the narrative. One of those forms comes out of the desert tradition of Israel and is called the Tent of Meeting tradition. It was something celebrated in the later history of the Hebrew people, a ceremony through which ancient nomadic folk from the wilderness believed that God was coming to them in the form of a cloud. That image can be seen clearly in this Sinai experience.

The other narrative form is from the settled tradition of Israel that developed after the people took root in Canaan. It is called the Covenant Renewal ceremony, the means whereby the people of Israel gathered annually in worship on a particular day to renew their Covenant. It was this ceremony of renewal, about which the people of Israel knew a great deal, that provides the context or the form which they read back into their account of the original Covenant experience.

Interwoven in this text is the Yahwist document's emphasis on royalty, which competes with the Elohist antiroyalist emphasis. For example, the Yahwist version seems to be present in the story where Moses is elected, chosen, and authenticated by God himself, where Moses is appointed by God as the intercessor on behalf of the people. Moses is the voice through which God speaks.

The Elohist version, which is much more democratic, is heard where the people elect Moses to be their representative. The power continues to reside in the people's selection, not in God's special election of Moses. One must remember that the Yahwist document comes to us out of the southern kingdom, which had the royal line of David as its dominant institution, while the Elohist version comes out of the north, where there never was an established royal line, and where the people were constantly rebelling against the southern tradition that wanted to impose the southern king upon the northern region. The Yahwist document reveals what might be called a catholic emphasis: God acted through the hierarchy to reach the people. The Elohist document reveals a much more Protestant one: God spoke directly to the people, who then elected their representatives.

There are some other differences. The Yahwist version pictures God as descending upon the mountain, causing it to smoke and shake like a volcano. The Elohist version assumes that God lives on this mountain, concealed in the thunderclouds that are always present there. In the Yahwist version, the Covenant is made with Moses, who mediates it to the people. In the Elohist version, the Covenant is made with the people, who elect Moses to represent them for purposes of negotiation.

We need also to note that in many ways Sinai is where the history of Israel begins. A case could be made that the first real chapter of the Old Testament, in terms of history, is Exodus Nineteen. Before Sinai, before Exodus Nineteen, the Hebrew people were an escaping band of slaves; but after Sinai they were a holy nation, a people of destiny, a nation of priests ordained to serve the world. They were chosen to be a people who were identifiable in history by their Covenant.

Only after Sinai did the people of Israel look back at Egypt and see the hand of God bringing them out of captivity and into this moment of Covenant. More specifically, only after Sinai did they develop the folklore of their ancient heroes—Abraham, Isaac, Jacob, and Joseph—legends of whom contain a germ of history but are mostly self-serving folklore designed to prove that this slave people's ancestry was in fact not slavery but nobility and also to prove that this nomadic nation had a legitimate claim to that land which they were in fact dedicated to taking by military might.

In a sense, the whole history of Israel thus begins at Sinai, and whatever occurred before is the remembered folklore that brings the Hebrew people to this moment. After Sinai they begin the self-conscious history of seeking to live out what it means to be the Covenant people.

It is also at this point that one of the tensions that marks the historic life of Israel and later marks the life of the Christian Church, which claims to be the new Israel, first becomes obvious. It is a wrenching tension upon which the whole story of

the Bible might be told. It is best articulated in questions—
how do you have a sense of being chosen by God and at the
same time avoid the sense of feeling that to be the chosen
people somehow makes you superior to all other people? Is
Israel's call or the Christian Church's call a call to a privileged
status, or is it a call to a life of service? Is it a possession to be
made exclusive, or is it to be inclusive? Is the Covenant to be
open to all people, or is it to be closed to all but the privileged
few?

Throughout biblical history this tension is ever present.
First one side is dominant and then the other, until finally the
image of exclusivity and privilege manages to prevail, setting
the stage for a rending apart of Jew from Christian. I think the
crucial time comes in the period of the Exile when the people
of Israel have a chance to go back to their homeland. Under
the leadership of Nehemiah and Ezra they begin to build an
exclusive, externally righteous group, with which no one can
be identified unless he or she conforms to certain external
standards. It is this attitude that is challenged deeply within
Israel by the prophetic writings of Second Isaiah. He says the
role of the holy people of God is to bring life and love into the
world through even their own suffering. "A light to lighten
the Gentiles" is the way glory is brought to Israel, he proclaims as a lonely voice in the wilderness. However, the Nehe-
miah-Ezra attitude meets the status needs of an insecure nation, and soon it is legitimized in organized religion, finally
resulting in the people mentioned in the New Testament, who
have turned the worship of Yahweh into a rigid moralistic and
ecclesiastical system. The Pharisees we see in the Gospels
were good men; they were morally righteous people. They
were the pillars of society. They were the keepers of the Law,
but they acted as though to be a Pharisaic Jew was to possess
status that gave them importance beyond anyone else. They
called upon that status as a way of proving their superiority
and consequently everyone else's inferiority. Many times they
were blinded by their own sense of external righteousness to
the human need in everyone for love, acceptance, forgiveness,
and community. In many senses, it is this attitude that was
challenged and confronted by Jesus of Nazareth acting very

much in the tradition of the lonely and unknown voice we have named Second Isaiah. The battle still goes on from generation to generation in both Judaism and Christianity.

Jesus challenged the prevailing vision of the Covenant as exclusive, self-fulfilling, ego building. He challenged it in the name of a call to service, openness, love, and to the vocation of giving life and love away, which becomes the Christian vocation. He challenged its exclusivity in the name of all humankind, by seeing that the love, power, forgiveness, and acceptance of God literally melts all of the barriers of exclusiveness. The Covenant, he maintained, is finally beyond all external judgments of race, sex, and ethnic origin.

Christianity is born in this moment and out of this attitude. Yet the same thing has happened to the Christian Church through the ages that happened in the Jewish tradition. We Christians who claim to serve this inclusive power of love that we see in Jesus the Christ have corrupted that Christian calling into a position serving our own sense of superiority, our life of status. We have developed in our tradition a privileged priesthood. We have institutionalized our Gospel, and as soon as we institutionalize it, we discover that we have corrupted it. Institutionalization is essential for any movement to live in history, but all institutions become corrupt. The only way an institutionalized Gospel can live is to have constant reformation. Whenever it gets socked into concrete, it becomes distorted. As soon as Christianity became institutionalized, we Christians began to require acquiescence to creeds and conformity in worship before people could be members. The result has been that in the name of creeds and conformity Christians have battered one another in religious wars, in inquisitions, in heresy trials. The God of love is never served by a rejecting community dedicated to the proposition that they, and they alone, are the only true believers, the only pure worshipers, the only proper Christians. Yet our history is full of that attitude. The Jews saw themselves as the chosen people. So do the Christians. But we Christians, like the Jews, are chosen to be the agents of the God of life and love. We are not chosen so that we can stand in judgment upon those we regard to be less enlightened, less insightful, or less faithful to a specific understanding of the revelation of God.

Sinai is the place where this tension between privilege and service first comes into focus for the Hebrew people.

The last point in Exodus Nineteen that casts light upon our understanding of the Ten Commandments is the biblical concept of the otherness of God. When God, in the Bible, is perceived to be present on a mountain, he is an awesome, fearful, holy presence. The Hebrews have chosen their images from the analogy of a volcano. Thus, they portray God in terms of unrestrained power, smoke, thunder, lightning, and the shaking of the ground underneath their feet. The sound of the ram's horn rises to an ear-splitting intensity. Those are the words they use, the feelings, the thoughts, and the concepts which they employ when they begin to talk or write about the presence of God. There is connected with this imagery a kind of compelling terror. The Hebrews are caught in this experience. In their fear they want to flee, but in their yearning to be brought into the life of this God, they cannot turn their eyes away; they are mesmerized.

When Moses walks from the people into the cloud, he is legitimized as God's special instrument. When he comes back to the people, he is covered with God's transforming glory, so that the brightness of Moses' face literally must be shielded unless the people be blinded.

It is in this setting, with this sense of the otherness, the holiness of God, that the Law is given. The Law is clothed with solemnity, with divinity, and with a self-authenticating power. That is the context in which the duty of a human being toward his God and the duty of a human being toward his neighbor is spelled out.

Forget for a moment the literal symbols. Forget whether they come from volcanoes or desert thunderstorms or whatever. It is not where the Hebrew people got their symbols that matters, but why they chose those particular symbols. Get underneath the symbols and capture the feelings. God, to the Hebrews, is not a permissive pop, a sweet daddy up in the sky. To the Hebrews, to the whole biblical mind, God is a Holy Other who binds his people into Covenant, a Covenant that makes demands and brings judgment, calling them into responsible freedom and setting guidelines. Election by this holy God brings no special status, no privileged position. It certainly does not promise wealth and success; indeed it may bring pain and persecution. As one rabbi said to me one time, "I'd love for somebody else to be the chosen people for just a generation." The election by this holy God to this Covenant status is, rather, a call of this people to share God's work of redemption, to bear up under the righteous demands of God, and to accept the abuse of the world. One does not enter that experience lightly.

The Bible is quite emphatic about fear being a necessary part of the human covenant relationship with God. God and fear are never separated biblically. That separation is a modern, twentieth-century idea. But biblical fear is not the fear that a child might have quaking before an angry parent. It is, rather, the fear that comes in the sense of recognizing that there is a holy claim being made upon our lives, a demand being made upon our behavior, a mystical power present that we can never control, tame, or manipulate. Until we grasp this sense of God, so vividly portrayed in the preclude to the Ten Commandments, I do not believe that we can say we have ever experienced the biblical God. No element of God's nature is more foreign to our generation than these elements of power —otherness, holiness, wonder, awe, and fear.

The glory and the holiness of the God of Mount Sinai calls forth in the Covenant people awe, wonder, and fear, which is expressed, finally, in their obedience to those principles through which God's presence is seen in human life, those principles through which life, love, and the fullness of God's creation are finally achieved.

This is not a pleasure ethic. This is not the kind of ethic that says we can do what we want so long as we can get away with it. It is a holy demand that should not be lightly ignored. It has to do with our deepest commitment, with our character and with our standards of behavior. One can live a righteous life externally without worshiping God, but one cannot worship God without having that worship express itself in the righteousness of one's behavior.

The biblical Covenant is God's invitation to a people to come and live in the fullness of life. It is an expression of the love of God seen as God's election. It is grace. As soon as the grace of election is experienced, then the biblical law which defines the holiness that is demanded of the Covenant people is immediately given. If you have law without the graceful covenant, you are caught in an empty legalism; but if you have the graceful covenant, the sense of election, without the content of the law, you will never endure, for that would be cheap grace, and the Bible does not know cheap grace. It only knows the costliness of discipleship.

The New Testament does not substitute a friendly God, a permissive or sweet doting daddy in the sky, for the awe, wonder, holiness, and terror of Mount Sinai. What the New Testament does do is to portray the gracious message of an open access to that same God whose depth of accepting love is seen on a cross and whose presence in the life of that crucified one is designed to call forth from us the same awe, reverence, and obedience to those rules of life through which we find the fullness of life, the depth of love, and the meaning of our own humanity.

We now turn to examine the content of the demands of the Holy God who spoke from the mysterious Mount Sinai.

3

The Commandments—
Some General Observations

The best known part of the Book of Exodus is the Ten Commandments. Many a Sunday school pupil has committed them to memory. To many adults they seem to be vastly important as a moral standard even if these same adults are not certain of their specific content. I remember well a moment in my ministry when this fact became obvious. I was serving a suburban congregation of rather socially prominent, conservative Episcopalians in a small southwestern Virginia city. In that parish there was general criticism of our church school program because it was said we did not "teach the Bible" specifically enough. Somehow all of the problems of the teenagers were blamed on the fact that the churches no longer stuck to the basics. At a lively social event one evening a woman whose daughter was not exactly on the straight and narrow came up to me holding a drink that was obviously not her first of the evening. This was the moment she had picked to lecture me on the failure of the Church to give proper instruction and moral guidance to the emerging generation. Her strongest and most self-evident point was that children no longer had to learn the Ten Commandments. Being possessed at such moments by what is obviously a demonic spirit, I replied, "Do you know the Ten Commandments?" "Of course," she responded, somewhat angry that I had dared to ask. "Name them," I challenged. There was a cough, a sputter, an angry look, and finally she remembered adultery and murder! The conversation terminated rather abruptly, and so did her good opinion of me, assuming she had ever had one in the first place.

In this volume we will probe the meaning of those Ten Commandments on two levels. First, we will seek to get underneath the words to gaze at the eternal truth they embody. Second, we will explore their application to the complexities of life in the twentieth century.

We begin with a brief look at history. How did these ten precepts come to occupy so central a position in both Hebrew and Christian thought? What was their early cultic meaning? How did the scope of the Commandments expand? What do they mean today? Are these ancient words still relevant for our generation, or for our century? These are the questions this chapter will seek to address.

Let me first clearly state the obvious. The Ten Commandments, like the Bible, did not drop from heaven fully written. This is very difficult for many people to comprehend, for I recall vividly how this biblical episode was treated in Cecil B. De Mille's *The Ten Commandments*.

To me the most offensive moment in that extravaganza was the portrayal of the giving of those Commandments. God was pictured as a divine drill or a magic buzz saw. Moses held two tablets of stone up and the fiery finger of God attacked them, writing out the Ten Commandments in perfect Hebrew. That is never the way ethical systems are born or cultural taboos formulated, nor is that the way the Ten Commandments came into being. God did not write the Bible. God did not dictate the Ten Commandments. Only the naiveté of biblical literalism would allow anyone to think that.

The Bible and the Ten Commandments came out of the living, moving, worshiping, insightful life of the Hebrew nation. This nation was the product of a particular worldview. They captured insights that are limited by time and conditioned by history. They failed to understand many of the realities of our day because they could not in their wildest imaginations have envisioned our complex world. Eighth-century B.C. Hebrews, for example, could not have embraced the contemporary medical technology that would enable life to continue after humanity in any recognizable form had ceased to exist. Neither could they envision the intense complications of trying to relate that modern circumstance to the Commandment "You shall not kill." When the Hebrew people talked about adultery, they were living in a culture where marriage followed very shortly after puberty, within one year at the maximum. They could not have imagined a civilization such as ours that has separated puberty from marriage by ten to fifteen years. Hence, the standards in their world, when literalized or universalized, create problems in our world that are real and must be explored.

There is a second difficulty. The earliest written document in the Old Testament is the Yahwist document. As noted before, the Yahwist document achieved written form about the year 950 B.C., but the historic Moses dates from between 1400 to 1250 B.C., which means that at the minimum there is a three-hundred-year gap between historic Moses and the first writing of the code of the Ten Commandments. During this time, the oral tradition of the Hebrew people was the only vehicle for passing on tradition. The Elohist document, which is the second oldest document and which constitutes the bulk of the familiar version of the Ten Commandments found in Exodus Twenty, was written around 750 B.C. This brings an even deeper complication, for it means that by the time the version of the Ten Commandments with which you and I are familiar was actually written, five hundred years had elapsed from the time that they were purported to have been given. For five hundred years the Sinai tradition and the Ten Commandments circulated in oral form, being changed and conditioned by the living events of the history of the Hebrew people. Only when the Hebrews began to write their code down did they enshroud it in divinity, engrave it in stone, and claim that God himself had spoken or written these laws for them.

Obviously the Ten Commandments had a long history of development. There was no instantaneous creation of these words. There are three distinct and different versions of the Ten Commandments in the Old Testament. There is Exodus Twenty, the familiar form which is basically from the Elohist document with some Priestly interpolations. There is a version in Exodus Thirty-four, which is basically from the Yahwist document and which is almost totally cultic and not ethical, having to do with worship forms, not behavior. The third version is in Deuteronomy Five, which is basically the Deuteronomic version and is similar to Exodus Twenty.

These three separate accounts only prove that there was a long period of oral tradition and development. There was not even agreement on the number ten or on which commandments constituted the ten, to say nothing of lack of consensus on the content itself. There was much editorializing. We can see where commandments have been expanded with editorial comment, such as all that explanatory detail about who the Sabbath day observance really affects. There are also places where the commandments actually seem to have been shortened, although that is not quite so easy to document.

The ethical norms by which any people live are, I believe, finally rooted in and ultimately grow out of that people's economic struggle for survival. For example, in the nineteenth century we of the West began to be aware of other cultures, of other peoples and civilizations around the world, in a way that had not before been part of our consciousness. It suddenly became very popular in intellectual circles to assert that morals were relative and that there were no absolutes. In many ways that is correct. The ethical content of the moral code of a people varies widely from civilization to civilization, from society to society. We have only to look at so basic a pattern of human life as marriage. There are peoples whose sense of morality in marriage has been asserted inside an institutional shape that was polygamous, polyandrous, and monogamous. The content varied widely. The Bible itself said that polygamy was all right or else Solomon was Exhibit A of a biblical sex fiend. Try to imagine a man who had 300 wives and 700 concubines being extolled as the virtue of wisdom!

There are also civilizations where the elderly were honored and revered, even worshiped. In other civilizations the elderly were encouraged to die, even banished from the tribe to certain death. Yet both civilizations regarded their behavior as moral.

In our country, in our own brief two-hundred-year history, the moral code has changed dramatically. The factor forcing change has not been some immoral revolution. Rather it has been the reality of the economic struggle for survival in this country. We were at one time a frontier nation but now we are largely an urban megalopolis. Large families in the day of the frontier were smiled upon as the blessing from God. Infant mortality and the death of women in childbirth was a constant reality. To do the work of taming the frontier required large families for survival and economic well-being, and so the moral code blessed that tradition. Today all of that has changed. Now large families are viewed as an act of irresponsible parenthood in an overcrowded, frontierless world facing a shortage of food that reaches starvation levels. Large families or those unwilling to limit birth or population appear to be the immoral ones or at least the morally irresponsible ones. This is a radical shift in ethical understanding and at rock bottom, it clearly rises out of our economic struggle for survival.

Ethics are the very stuff of life. Ethics are the rules which we create to live together in some kind of harmony. They rise out of common consent from within the people, from within the special and peculiar life circumstances of that people. The ethics that become the rules of our common life have to be generally accepted. They have to be pragmatic and practical. They have to function. Ethics have the purpose of protecting people from each other; when they work they help build in society a dignity, a personal integrity, and even a divinity because there must be some sense of the sacred to keep that population living in a creative way. It is at that point, out of common consent, that the ethical standards and norms are written down as laws. They are codified; they are elevated to be the expression of the absolute will of the divinity; and they are enshrouded with the concept of worship. They are regarded as God's rules, written to govern human life. Finally, a tradition inevitably develops that tells the story of how these rules were first received, a story which roots them not in the common life of the people, but in the element of the divine. That is the normal process that has taken place in every civilization and is very probably the way the story told in Exodus Twenty came into being.

Exodus Twenty is not the only codification of rules in the Old Testament. It is simply the most popular and the best known. There is also in the Pentateuch a group of codified laws called the Book of the Covenant. In the Book of Leviticus another group of laws is called the Holiness Code. Neither achieved popularity. The Ten Commandments are clearly the most familiar set of rules and, in the life of the Hebrew people, they obviously became the most important. Christianity simply took them over.

Some general comments about the Ten Commandments must be made before moving to the particularity of the first one. To give a certain symmetry, I will offer ten general observations about the Ten Commandments.

1. The Ten Commandments are mostly negative. Depending on how you count the Commandments, either seven or eight are "no" or "you shall not" Commandments, and only two at the minimum and three at the maximum are positive statements.

Negatives tend to set the boundaries on human behavior, and to curb irresponsible action. Negatives cannot make you love your neighbor, but they certainly can curb the hate and the way you express your lack of love for your neighbor. Negatives also assume that human nature is not capable of behaving with nobility. To state the Commandments negatively recognizes that human nature expresses a *fallen* status, that human beings are creatures who need to have clear boundaries set around their behavior. In terms of the way we normally count the Commandments, only the observance of the Sabbath Day and the injunction to honor your parents come across as positive statements.

2. The Ten Commandments purport to have been given by God and yet after the first two, the text of the narrative shifts from God speaking in the first person to God speaking in the third person. In the first two Commandments God says, "I am," and after that he is simply called the Lord. This is either a tacit agreement that God did not dictate these Commandments or else God's sense of grammar is a bit confused. Interestingly enough, the addressee of the Commandment is always the second person singular, *"you* shall not," *"you* shall," and that second person singular is not often found in a legal series in this period of history.

3. From time to time, motivational clauses seem to have been added. For example, why should you honor your parents? So your days may be long. The Commandment gives you a motivation. Why should you not take the Lord's name in vain? So

that you can avoid being held guilty for that offense. None of these motivational clauses seems to be original.

4. Exactly how the Commandments are counted has never been consistent. Actually there are only nine injunctions, not ten. The first Commandment is divided in order to make two and arrive at the sacred number ten. "You shall have no other gods" and "You shall make no graven images," are both a part of the same Commandment. The Roman Catholic and Lutheran Churches combined these into one as they originally were. When they reached the end they had only nine, so they split the tenth one and made two injunctions against coveting, which makes it appear that coveting is an especially large problem among Roman Catholics and Lutherans. Actually in Jewish commentaries, where the law is broken into 613 separate injunctions, the Ten Commandments constitute fifteen, not ten, of the 613 injunctions. They are numbers twenty-five through thirty-nine of the Torah, and the first Commandment is not the one about having no other gods at all. It is rather a statement on the "being" of God which will be considered later.

5. The biblical tradition about the two tablets of stone does not appear in the Bible in conjunction with the familiar version of the Ten Commandments that is in Exodus Twenty. The Exodus Twenty account has no version of two tablets of stone whatsoever. The tablet tradition is attached to Exodus Thirty-four and the Deuteronomic version in Deuteronomy Five. There is no biblical suggestion as to how these Commandments should be divided into two groups on the two tablets. It was only a later tradition that tended to see the first tablet as our duty to God and the second tablet as our duty toward our neighbor.

6. Every one of the Ten Commandments can be found elsewhere in the corpus of the Torah in the Old Testament. They are not mentioned solely in this familiar list. If every list of the Ten Commandments were destroyed, we could create the ten out of the rest of the Pentateuch. Indeed the Ten Commandments seem to be the barest distillation of the essence of the Law, both cultic and ethical. This suggests that the whole law was given first and that these ten rose to

the surface and were codified later out of the larger corpus.

7. The Ten Commandments themselves contain no sanctions or specific punishments for violations. However, in other places in the Old Testament the death penalty is prescribed for violating injunctions such as murder and adultery. We run into that in the New Testament when the woman caught in the act of adultery is being taken out to the edge of the city to be executed by stoning before Jesus intervenes. The would-be stoners quote Moses as their justification for condemning her to death.

8. The Ten Commandments are marked by a stark objectivity in the present form. I suspect that their original shape, once they reached a recognizable form distinct from the larger corpus of the Law, was something like this:

1. I am Yahweh.
2. You shall have no other gods before me.
3. You shall not take the name of the Lord in vain.
4. Remember to keep holy the Sabbath day.
5. Honor your father and your mother.
6. You shall not kill.
7. You shall not commit adultery.
8. You shall not steal.
9. You shall not bear false witness.
10. You shall not covet.

I suspect the reason that ten became the holy number is nothing more sacred than that we have ten fingers on our hands and that made it easy to teach children the essence of the moral code of the Hebrew people.

The Ten Commandments in the biblical narrative are very brief, very succinct, and easily memorized. There is no room for discussion, no room for modern, post-Freudian emphasis upon the motivation that elicits the particular behavior, and no room for considering all the extenuating circumstances. They are blunt, dogmatic, and straightforward in the biblical form.

9. In the final form of the Old Testament, the Ten Commandments are given a special place and a very special name.

To the Jews they were the Ten Words. They are the touch-stone and the foundation of the Covenant. They have a final-ity. "These words spake Yahweh, and he spoke no more," assert the Jews. The Ten Words, the Ten Commandments, are reflected in the prophets. They are enumerated in the books of Hosea and Jeremiah; they are mentioned in Psalms 50 and 81. It is clear that they came into the liturgical worship of the Hebrew people. In the final text of the Pentateuch the Com-mandments are placed in the position of being the very first words of God that come out of the theophany. The Ten Com-mandments are the first words to be heard by the Hebrew people gathered at Sinai. It was out of the smoke, fire, cloud, lightning, thunder, earthquake, mystery, magnetism, wonder and awe that accompanied the experience of Israel before that mountain that these Commandments were heard. By the time the writings of the Old Testament were being put into final form, they had assumed a place of preeminence in the life of the Hebrew nation.

10. Finally, it is assumed that the Ten Commandments re-flect the essential character of God himself. As the story is told in Exodus both the manner of delivery and the effect upon the hearers makes that point quite clear. Thus the Decalogue is set apart from the rest of the Law even though all the Law was thought to be from God. The Decalogue was the first among equals because these were God's first words to his people upon entering the Covenant.

God's mighty act of deliverance immediately called forth an ethical response from his people. Worship and behavior were never separated for the Hebrew. The negative tone of the Commandments set the outer limits of the Covenant. To vio-late these rules, these Commandments, to transgress these lim-its would set one outside the established life of the Covenant's people. Obviously to transgress these boundaries was not a misdemeanor, it was breaking the very fiber of which the divine-human relationship consisted.

The positive Commandments, which have to do with the being of God, the day of God, and the name of God, set the positive inner content for life in that Covenant. The God of the Covenant laid claim upon his people pointing them to a new life and a new destiny. The crossing of the Red Sea* was an act of grace. They, through no fault of their own, through no merit of their own, were chosen. They, who were no people, even slave people, the dregs of society, were elected and given value by God himself. That is the Red Sea experience; that is grace. Sinai was the act of response. Those who are loved, those who are chosen and given a sense of their dignity and worth, decide now that they will live this choice out in obedience. The elect people stand before Sinai to hear what election demands of them.

---

*Recent biblical scholarship has cast doubt on whether it was the Red Sea or the Sea of Reeds.

4

I Am Yahweh

The first Commandment according to the Jewish number-ing system is not a commandment at all. That is, we with our legalistic Western minds would never see a commandment in these words because they contain no injunction as to what we should or should not do. For this reason, Western Christians have tended to treat what the Jews considered as the first of the holy Ten Words as if it were a prologue rather than an integral part of the Decalogue. Yet if we would understand the impact of these laws, we must deal with what the Jews be-lieved was the first and, therefore, the most important Com-mandment.

"I am Yahweh who brought you out of the land of Egypt and out of the House of Bondage." To the Jewish mind the statement about God's being constitutes a commandment to believe, which is nothing less than a command to acknowledge the reality of God's total claim upon their lives. God is not an impersonal power, an "it" to the Jewish mind. Neither is God identified with nature, reason, fate, or with any philosophical concept. God is the source of life, the source of consciousness, the source of personality, moral purpose, and ethical action.

God is beyond time, beyond space, so the Jewish Psalmist could write, "If I go into heaven, you are there. If I go into hell, you are also there. If I take the wings of the morning and dwell in the uttermost parts of the sea, even there shall you find me." God is beyond all the human limits of time and space; God is in the heights and in the depths of life, but most uniquely to the Jewish people and the Jewish mentality, God is Yahweh, the Lord of history. Here at the heart of the Law, the affirma-tion about the God of the Covenant is not "I am Yahweh, the

Creator of Heaven and Earth." It is not, "I am Yahweh, Lord of Nature." That would be distant, inimitable, impersonal, and that is not the Jewish focus. Rather it is, "I am Yahweh, who acts in history. I act to free slaves, to bring justice. I act to give life. I am Yahweh whose love embraces the lowly and the downtrodden, the powerless. My love calls them into life. I am seen in the destinies of human beings. I am revealed in historic deeds. I act and you respond. I love before you deserve. Because I act and because I love, you are called to respond in love."

Obedience is not a duty, not even in the Old Testament. Obedience is the response of a grateful recipient to the infinite love of Yahweh. The Covenant people are not called to keep the Commandments in order to win God's love. They are called to keep the Commandments because God has already loved them. It is a eucharistic or thanksgiving effort and they keep the Commandments because they yearn in some way to respond to this infinite, loving, graceful God. The Old Testament is not law as opposed to the New Testament's grace. That is a Christian corruption of the Old Testament, an attempt to denigrate our Jewish heritage. God does not change. The God of Jesus of Nazareth is still the God of Moses. The Jews took the Sinai Covenant and legalized it making a reformation and a challenge essential. Christians have likewise taken the Gospels and legalized them. That is the human corruption of the grace of God and it is both a Jewish and Christian distortion of the biblical meaning. The biblical injunction is clear and consistent: God is; God loves; God acts; God frees. We respond; we worship; we obey; we live in the glorious liberty of the children of God. We then join this God in the act of loving and freeing those who are in the chains and bonds and shackles of human corruption.

I am Yahweh. That is the first Commandment. I am the God who brought you out of Israel. History is my arena. Incarnation is my *modus operandi*. Revelation in the concrete events of life is my style. I call Abraham to leave Ur of the Chaldees to form a new historic people. I choose Isaac over Ishmael, Jacob over Esau. I work through the human family to accomplish my purposes. I can redeem the evil motives of my own human creation. The human jealousy of Joseph's brothers causes them to sell him into slavery. I make even that evil serve my purposes. From birth I prepare those who will serve my will. Pharaoh, mighty by earthly standards, becomes a mere pawn in my plans for the destiny of my world. I lead my people out of slavery into freedom. I am involved in their lives. I raise up prophets to speak my word. I work even through those who do not know my name. Cyrus of the Persians is my agent in the drama of salvation. If you want to find me, you must look at life and history. I come calling my creation to respond, to live, to love, to be. The holiness of life, the fullness of being, the presence of God are always seen in the living out of a perfect historic destiny in obedience to my will, which is seen in the midst of life in my creation. I am being. I am life. I am love. I am Yahweh. The great I AM is my name. My name reveals my nature. You are my people.

The first Commandment is simply a commandment to hear God's being, to acknowledge God's sovereignty, and to admit God's total claim on all of life. Thus for the Hebrew, how we worship and how we live are indivisible. And for Jesus, loving God, loving our neighbor, and loving ourselves becomes the summary upon which hangs all the Law and the prophets.

I am Yahweh. Hear and respond.

5

No Other Gods

What the Jews call the second Commandment, Christians tend to divide into two parts, some making it Commandments one and two. The text is simple and quite familiar: You shall have no other gods before me. You shall not make to yourself any graven image or the likeness of anything that is in heaven above or in the earth beneath or in the waters under the earth. You shall not bow down to them nor worship them. For I, the Lord your God, am a jealous God. I visit the iniquity of the fathers upon the children to the third and fourth generation of those who hate me but showing steadfast love to the thousands of those who love me and keep my commandments.

Notice that this Commandment is in the first person, for this is the last time the first person is used in the Commandments; after this, God does not speak as the "I," but is spoken about as "the Lord."

Analyzing the Commandment from a form-critical point of view, we find it is really three interrelated injunctions. They all mean substantially the same thing: You shall have no other gods; you shall make no images; you shall worship nothing less than God. Then there is added a rather long explanation of God's nature. This constitutes the fullness of that Commandment. It is rich in theological insight, profound in its penetration into the meaning of life itself, and exciting to seek to understand. You might be surprised to discover that it is also very controversial.

In many ways this Commandment transcends the limitations of time, space, and the outlook of the first century. First consider it in its biblical context and then in its expanded version.

Exodus Nineteen describes the setting: Israel, the former slave people, encamped at the foot of Mount Sinai. Somehow they believed themselves led to this particular, specific place, for in their minds this was the mountain of God. The people, standing at the foot of this mountain, were embraced, says the text, with "a holy fear" that made them receptive to the word of the Lord. In this setting, God spoke what the Torah regards as his holiest words. The first, as the Torah would list the Commandments, is a simple proclamation of his being: "I am," he said. It is not, for the Hebrew, a subject for debate. "I am" is a statement of the fact of God's being. "I am Yahweh." With that statement God makes an implicit claim for sovereignty over all of life.

Then the words move on. "Because I am," the second Commandment follows naturally, "I am the truth that fills the universe. I am the final reality so you can have no other gods. I am infinite so you can make no graven images and pretend that something you make might encompass my being. I am ultimate. You shall not bow down or worship anything less than the great *I am, Yahweh.*"

This Commandment is a double-edged sword because it is first a literal statement meaning exactly what it says; and second, it is a sweeping, probing, almost unfathomable message, searching the deepest recesses of human life.

This is not a Commandment given much attention today, for idolatry is not considered a major temptation of our time. Very little do we understand the meaning of idolatry!

Paul Tillich, a great theologian of the twentieth century, defined God as a person's ultimate concern. Your God is that reality which elicits from you your deepest feelings and your most ultimate concern, he said. If that Tillichian definition is accepted, then there is no such thing as an atheist, for every life has an ultimate concern. Every life has a god. The question is not, Is there a god for you? but What kind of god does your life serve? What is the nature of your ultimate concern? Is it personal or non-personal? Does your ultimate concern give you slavery or freedom? Does it give you death or life? Does it open you to all that life has, or does it push you out of existence? Looking at life through these eyes, we can see that our world is no less polytheistic than in the days when the Ten Commandments were being composed. The only difference is that we are a little more sophisticated about our idols and about our gods. Ask yourself these questions, and then you will know where your idols are: Where is your ultimate loyalty? What is the ultimate value your life is organized to serve? Where does your security rest? Where can you be most deeply threatened? What does your money finally support? On an even deeper level, does your life serve a unified whole? Or are you split up in divergent, competitive values, serving all sorts of conflicting goals. If God is one, then there must be a unity that comes to our lives by the worship of that oneness. If God is one, then our lives must reflect one standard, one value, one truth, and one love that is ultimate. That finally will result in one human family, not a family where everybody looks alike, acts alike, or understands the truth in the same way, but one family all drawn into unity by the worship of one God.

If God is a unity for us, then there cannot be one law that applies to people we like and another law that applies to those we don't like. There cannot be one value by which we relate to our families and another value by which we relate to strangers. There cannot be one code which governs our countrymen and another code which governs aliens. If the God of life is one, and if the God of life is seen in every child of his creation, then we must treat every child of his creation as if that child is holy, and there can be no categorical denial of another's sacred humanity. If God is one there can be no slavery. If God is one, there can be no segregation. If God is one, there can be no prejudice and no bigotry, for every act of discrimination, whether it is economic, political, or social, reveals that we have different standards by which we judge the creatures of God's creation. Every act of discrimination reveals that God is not one, and our lives are schizophrenic, for if the value we live out is not unified, then the God we worship is not one. We are serving other gods than Yahweh, the great I AM, the source of life, love, and being, the bringer of freedom. We are violating this Commandment.

If the God of life is seen in every child of his creation, there can be no distinction between those who fight on our side in a conflict and those who fight against us. When we depersonal-ize people to the point of rejoicing in their deaths, we are violating the oneness of God. To preserve our humanity in the face of our attitude toward people who in warfare we call our enemies, we try to act as if they are not really human. We depersonalize them through our propaganda in all kinds of ways. Those are not human beings who are brothers, fathers, or sons that we are killing in our wars; no, they are "Krauts," "Japs," "Chinks," "V.C.," communists or mercenaries. They are reduced to subhuman levels of life. All of those terms of personal disparagement that we employ allow us to kill and not violate our humanity. Whenever this attitude invades our lives, the oneness of God is compromised, and polytheism is apparent. Therefore one cannot listen to this Commandment without hearing judgment. "You shall have no other gods before me."

If God is one, then every war in human history is a civil war, for it is a war inside the family of God's people. If that is so, then our nation must be seen by the worshipers of Yahweh not as any more sacred, any more holy, or any more righteous than any other nation or people, and our propaganda that would try to convince us otherwise must be countered in the name of the oneness of God. That propaganda is especially vicious when we are involved in a foreign war; it is amazing that we do not realize what is happening to us. Somehow when we get into the conflict of a war, we have to choose sides. We do not stop to think that war itself is nothing but an instrument of our foreign policy. Our foreign policy is formulated by fallible, egocentric human beings who constitute our government and who inevitably are serving their scheme of values and their understanding of life.

When an administration makes a mistake in domestic pol-icy, criticism is free. Critics bring pressure upon that adminis-tration to change that policy; that is considered legitimate political dialogue. Yet when an administration makes a mis-take in foreign policy and embroils us in a war, suddenly those critics are called traitors; their patriotism is questioned. This can only be done in the name of a nationalistic idol that stands in the place of the one God, Yahweh.

Someone once asked Abraham Lincoln if he thought God

was on the side of the North in the Civil War. Mr. Lincoln responded, "The real question is not whether God is on our side but whether we are on God's side." If you suggest such a sentiment in a time of conflict, you will run the risk of being branded a coward or a traitor. If the flag of nationalism flies above the altar of God, we have become idolators. The worship of God calls us out of that narrow boundary by which we define the worth of human life; it calls us into a deeper understanding of the common humanity that binds us all. Nationalism is one of the idols that we have enshrined in the place where only God belongs.

This nation may well be the greatest nation upon the face of the earth, but don't misunderstand what I am saying. We cannot stand in the Judeo-Christian tradition unless we see this nation as always under judgment. Indeed, worshipers of Yahweh in every land must always see their nation as under that judgment. There are things more sacred than nationhood.

We render to Caesar the things that are Caesar's, but Caesar can never be the object of worship or we become idolators. "My nation, right or wrong," is okay by me, so long as I am free to say with my patriotism and my human integrity intact, "But in this instance my nation is wrong!" Those bumper stickers that proclaim "America, love it or leave it!" express idolatry. Because I love America I will be critical in the same way that a parent who though loving the child still judges the child's behavior according to certain noble standards.

God can never be the guarantor of the American way of life. God can never be used as the bulwark for democracy. God can never be the battler against communism, as if all evil resides there and all virtue is on the side of capitalism.

God *is*. That is what the Commandment says. God *is*. Only God is sufficient, whole, and complete, and only God is a unity that needs no ulterior motive. When God is used for ulterior purposes, we have created a god out of our own needs. Some aspects of our lives reveal that we have changed very little from the pagan days when there was a god who was served on each day, and each god had requirements that were different. The days of our week were named for gods. The sun god was the object of worship on Sunday. Thor, the god of war, was the god of Thursday, and so on.

We seek to use God in other ways, and whenever we succeed, we become idolators. God can never be used; this never works. The only way we can respond to God is in worship. We cannot isolate him and manipulate him. Prayer does not bring good luck. Worship does not guarantee success. Religion cannot be sought as the means to create family solidarity. Praying together will not guarantee that you stay together. Faith is never a tool or a means to gain something else, at least not faith in the God who is I AM, the God whose glory fills the world, the God whose life throbs in the life of every human being, the God whose love is the matrix of our world. God is. God alone is ultimate. God alone is real. God alone must be worshiped and adored. The God who is God can never be manipulated, measured, captured, or tamed.

That is what the second part of this Commandment goes on to say: you cannot make an image of this God. Don't limit that to simply building golden calves and icons that you can bow before in your home. That is not what this aspect of the Commandment means. It means that God can never be captured; God can never be seen. God can never be made to serve your needs or mine. No barriers of human life, no places of worship, no representation, no symbol, no sacrament can contain God. His beauty cannot be captured in any beauty of humanity—not in architecture, not in art. We can point to him, but we can never capture him. God's being can never be described, not in the Bible, not in a church, not in a denomination, not even in a creed. These are only symbols that point us to God but they never capture God. Thus no Bible can be worshiped nor can it be installed as the infallible revelation of the word of God, without falling into idolatry. No creed can finally define God. No denomination can finally capture truth; and when with our limited minds, we act as if one can, we become idolators.

The experience of worship is supposed to open life to the world, to call life to freedom, to accept life's diversity in the common quest after the oneness of God. Idolatry, on the other hand, is always closed and defensive, even imperialistic. Idolatry demands conformity. Idolatry will make us slaves to a system for it suggests that deviation from the system is deviation from God. God *alone* is real. God alone is truth. Even

Christianity only approximates God; it does not capture God. Christianity contains truth but it is not to be equated with truth. Christianity points to God but to the degree that it is a system devised by human beings, we must acknowledge that God is always beyond our human system. And if Christianity does not capture the truth of God, then surely neither does any individual branch or denomination of Christendom, despite the claims of little minds made through the centuries.

What arrogance marks our Christian history! We have taken our tiny little insights into the truth of God; we have elevated them to the place of God himself; we have thereby created an idol; and then we have taken our little idols and we have used them to club into submission those who do not agree with us. If they do not get clubbed into submission, we excommunicate them as heretics who no longer share the truth. We have blessed our inhuman behavior with religious phrases and religious jargon. It is neither a secret nor a mystery that even the Ku Klux Klan frequently invokes the name of God in the prejudice and venom which it spews out upon people.

We take our inhuman behavior; we bless it with religious phrases and religious jargon; then we beat on one another in the name of God so that Catholics and Protestants feel justified in killing each other in Ireland, and Christians and Moslems do likewise in Lebanon. Back on the ranch, mild sinners that we Episcopalians are, we content ourselves with simply living out our attitude of superiority. Few Episcopalians are committed enough to go out and fight a war over Episcopalianism. We are content to sit back and look down on everyone else. That too is idolatry.

You shall have no other gods but me. This is a call to live in responsible freedom. It is a call to live in this world without any certainty, without any ultimates, in the midst of life's unknown dimensions. It is a call to live in the world without the certainty that any word, any phrase, or any institution is finally eternal. It is a call to live without idols, to know that every revelation, including our Bible, our creed, our tradition, is but a shadow; it is but a pale replica of the glory of God that no image of human creation will ever capture. When we pretend that we have captured it in our forms we are idolators.

The Commandment continues: "I am a jealous God." *Jealous* is a wonderfully human word. Jealousy occurs when my fulfillment is threatened by someone else, when my place is taken by another. This Commandment is saying that God fills the universe, that God fills the deepest hunger in the human soul, that God fills the vacuum and the emptiness in the heart of human life, and his place cannot be preempted. If it is preempted, life is inevitably distorted.

A layman in the deep South once said to me, "There is a God-shaped hole in every life that nothing else will finally fit." When anything else is put there, life is distorted, bent, and twisted.

The order of creation is achieved when God is the vine and we are the branches, when God is the life-giving power and we are related to him in such a way that we expand and bloom, becoming full, free, whole, and real. If that central relationship is distorted, if we look to something less than God for our fulfillment, seeking affirmation on the level of status, wealth, social position, achievement, education, power, or whatever, then our human light will inevitably burn at a lower wattage; our being will be distorted.

Human ego needs are manifold. Insecurity is part of our humanity—self-negativity can always be excited and elicited. To be apart from God is to be less than we are for it is an attempt to fill ourselves with some lesser deity. That will inevitably distort us and make us slaves to a lesser humanity. We will always seek to affirm, justify, or to prove our worth as if we do not believe that our worth has been given to us in the act of creation. When you and I are not at one with the source of life and love and the infinite ground of being that we call God, then inevitably we are not at one with ourselves either. When we are not at one with ourselves, we will not be at one with anyone else. Something else has been installed where only God belongs, with the result that we become agents of distortion in life, for God is jealous. The distortions of life are visited upon us and upon our children to the third and fourth generations, for insecurity gives birth to insecurity. Human beings build themselves up by tearing other human beings down. That is the price of our insecurity. That is what makes life a jungle. I seek power by reducing you to powerlessness. If I have to prove my worth or demonstrate my value, then my concern is inevitably focused upon me. I am seeking your acknowledgment of my superiority and not so subtly announcing that you are not as superior, that you are somewhat less than I. It is this insecure being who character-izes humanity in general and every human life in particular. Our humanity is insecure because we are separated from God's infinite source of love. God is not at the center of our life; something less than God is. That is the human condition and out of it we yearn for completion even while we try to convince others that we have it. The Bible calls this human condition sin. In the Bible sin is not a deed; it is a description of human life separated from the love of God and experiencing the reality of lack of love, inadequacy, and insecurity, and seeking to create the missing ingredients ourselves and always at someone else's expense. Sin in the Bible is all around us. That is why this sin can affect generation after generation. My inadequately loved self will inevitably give off inadequate love, and that inadequate love will distort my children, who in turn will distort their children to the third and fourth generation.

This is not a simplistic, deed-oriented Commandment. It is not an expression of some divine injustice that would picture God punishing children for the sins of their fathers. This insight underlies the actions of human behavior, and it must be understood there. This Commandment says that our being, our very human being, is either a source of death or a source of life to the world. The one factor that makes the difference, the one factor that affects our being is God's position in the organization of our world. How adequately are we in touch with this infinite source of life? How alive are we? Are we burning at the full wattage of our created power?

The glory of God is seen in human life when we are being what we were created to be. God is the vine, the source of all that gives life. We are the branches, through whom God's life and power flows.

"You shall have no other gods before me. I am jealous. No one can take my place without distorting my creation." The sins of the fathers do get visited upon the children to the third and fourth generation, for sin is the distortion of life that always comes when God is not central. Yahweh's demand is unconditional, exclusive, uncompromising, total. It is his divine picture of the meaning of creation, showing us the way that life is supposed to be. The Commandment does not, however, empower us. It only makes us aware that we are not what we were created to be, and that is the final burden of the law. The law cannot empower, it can only judge. Liturgically, when this Commandment is read in services of worship, our response is "Lord, have mercy upon us."

You shall have no other gods. You shall make no graven images. What depth! We shall find these Commandments to be deeper than we have imagined time after time.

6

God's Holy Name

You shall not take the name of the Lord your God in vain, for the Lord will not hold him guiltless that takes his name in vain." This is the third great word which according to the Book of Exodus was uttered from the mysterious mountain of Sinai. It is spoken out of smoke and fire, cloud, thunder, lightning, and earthquake. The final editors of the Book of Exodus intended for this setting to remain awesome, wondrous, fearful; for these were the solemn words of the covenant which bound Yahweh to his people and his people to Yahweh.

Commandment number one announced the being of God: "I am Yahweh." Commandment number two exerted Yahweh's claim to absolute sovereignty: Yahweh shares his preeminence with no one, with no thing. Yahweh alone is ultimate and true and real. Yahweh can be identified with no human enterprise, no nation, no clan, no way of life, no inner desire. The exclusiveness of Yahweh's radical claim upon the people of the covenant calls us out of any symptom of manmade security. It calls us out of every system through which we define ourselves. It calls us to live in wondrous and fearful freedom under God alone. Yahweh makes less than ultimate every other allegiance we have.

Yahweh is one. Yahweh is holy. Yahweh is true. There shall be no other gods, and no images, religious forms, or traditions shall be tolerated as symbols through which we pretend that we have captured the essence of God. That is the second word.

Then the third word is heard: Yahweh's name is holy. It must not be taken in vain. It must not be spoken in falsehood, for God will not hold guiltless one who takes that holy name in vain.

This Commandment is generally thought to be straightforward and not complex like so many of the others. Seen simplistically, it has been the text for stirring oratory from many a pulpit on the evils of profanity, even though it has almost nothing to do with profanity.

One of my favorite stories is about the great American preacher Harry Emerson Fosdick. Dr. Fosdick was invited to speak to a very hostile and tough group of striking coal miners in West Virginia. The miners had a habit of baiting preachers. Fosdick had been warned that if he did not get the attention of his audience quite early, at the very beginning, he would be in for a most uncomfortable evening. So when Dr. Fosdick stood up in the public square to address his surly audience on a hot July night, he began his sermon in a rather startling fashion. "It's goddamn hot today," he said.

Suddenly that tough crowd of coal miners fell silent, their mouths dropped open, and they focused to see if they had really heard what they thought they had heard. Then, holding their attention, Fosdick continued, "That's what I heard a man say this morning," and from that beginning, Dr. Fosdick launched into a passionate denunciation of profanity as a violation of the third Commandment.

I daresay that if most people were asked to define the meaning of the third Commandment, they would think that it had to do with profanity, especially profanity that invokes the holy name of God. Yet the truth is that this note came into this Commandment very late in its history, and constitutes only a tiny segment of its meaning. But clearly the primary focus of this Commandment is not against profanity but against perjury. Its real significance focuses on the mystical meaning of a name in the mind of the Hebrews.

It was William Shakespeare who said "What's in a name? That which we call a rose, by any other name would smell as sweet." Nothing, however, intrigued the mind of the Hebrew people more than the concept of the meaning and power of a name. The word *name* appears in the Old Testament seven hundred and fifty times. Everything is in the name of Yahweh; this is one of the most-used phrases in the biblical vocabulary. In the Book of Psalms alone, the phrase "the name of the

Lord" occurs ninety-eight times. To the Hebrew mind, the name of the Lord was holy and powerful. Beyond that, the Hebrews thought the name by which anything was called was significant, an omen. A name was not only a title; the name itself had mystery, power, and substance. It was a handle on the very being of the person.

Throughout the biblical story you will discover that the Bible is always careful to preserve a proper order about names, for to name someone or something was to assert that you had actual or potential power over that person or thing. Hence in the story of creation, God names Adam. Adam names the animals. Adam names Eve, for it was a patriarchal culture that wrote that story. Parents named their children. However, in the biblical story, no one could name God. Indeed, no one could even say that holy name. It was written as an un-pronounceable set of letters—YHWH—and when a Hebrew came upon that holy symbol in his scriptures, he did not read "Yahweh," as we might do, but he said the word *Adonai*, which literally means "my Lord." Hebrews were taught to say *Adonai* when they came to that holy symbol, lest they defile the holy name Yahweh by seeking to pronounce it.

In the Hebrew view of things, one's name participated in one's being. It was a clue to one's character. So in the biblical story, if your character changed, your name had to change also. When Abram was called out from Ur of the Chaldees to go into a strange land and give birth to a new nation, his name was changed from Abram to Abraham (Gen. 17:5). When Jacob wrestled with the angel of God by the brook Jabar, and crippled in that conflict became the father of a new people, his name was changed from Jacob to Israel (Gen. 35:10), and his descendants were called the "children of Israel." When Saul of Tarsus saw the light on the road to Damascus and had his life turned around, he became Paul, the apostle.*

Among the prophets of Israel, some would speak their prophetic word through the naming of their children. I think especially of First Isaiah (Isaiah 1–39). First Isaiah lived at a

---

*As a Roman citizen, Saul the Jew was likely always Paul the Roman; but Luke, reflecting the Hebrew idea, changes Saul to Paul in his text.

time when the enemies of Judah were about to crush this tiny nation. The little kingdom of Judah was wondering whether or not they would survive the Assyrian onslaught. So at that historic moment, Isaiah, the formost prophet in Jerusalem, named his firstborn son Shear-jashub, which meant "a remnant shall return": God will not allow his people of his Covenant to be annihilated. A prophetic word was thus spoken through a name.

A name for the Hebrews was a powerful symbol. When you called someone's name, you were claiming either superiority or equality. To have your name known by another was to reveal your character to another. All of this lies underneath the Hebrew attitude toward the name of God, the God who was mystery, the God who was ultimate, the God who was depth beyond penetration, height beyond perception, the God who was finally unknowable except that he chose to reveal as much of himself as his people could perceive. The Hebrews knew better than anyone else that the being of God was finally beyond every image, for he was reality beyond any godlike claim or any godly apprehension of his nature.

One of our hymns catches this Hebrew insight with these words:

> *Immortal, invisible God only wise,*
> *In light inaccessible hid from our eyes,*
> *Most blessed, most glorious, the ancient of days,*
> *Almighty victorious, thy great name we praise.*

It should not be surprising, given this background, that one of the Commandments deals with an attitude toward God's name. Nor should it be surprising that in the prayer Jesus himself gave us to pray, the very first petition says "Hallowed be your name."

This is necessary to understand as we turn specifically to this Commandment, for its primary focus, as I said earlier, is not against profanity but against perjury. It is an injunction against lying under oath.

According to the way a legal contract was made in ancient Israel, there was first of all a period of negotiation or bargaining—*haggling* might be a better word. When an agreement was reached the two contending parties would clasp hands and swear in the name of the Lord that they would be true to their word, that they would abide by their contract. Thus if they broke their word or if they violated their contract, if they did not live up to that oath, they had taken the name of the Lord in vain. That was the primary meaning of the Commandment. Basically this Commandment means, "Keep your word. Live up to your contracts. Don't swear in God's name to tell the truth and then tell less than the truth."

The word of a Hebrew, a member of God's covenanted people, was given in the name of the Lord, and that name stood for the whole being of God himself. Every word a member of the covenanted people spoke, every word of every Hebrew, was spoken under the oath of that covenant. A Jew's word was his honor, for it was bound by the name of Yahweh himself. To falsify one's word under oath—and the Hebrew in the covenanted community considered himself under oath all the time—was perjury. It was itself a crime for which one could be prosecuted. The Hebrews recognized that human honor and the ability to trust the integrity and the word of another were critical necessities in the life of a society. Without these basic realities, life itself was no longer trustworthy; it was reduced to a jungle warfare. Falsehood, deceit, and outright lies in the public or private arena shatter relationships and tear at the very fiber of human life. Truth and the integrity of one's word are essential to the hope of a nation, and leaders of that nation must embody that truth and integrity or the nation is morally bankrupt. Ability alone is not enough. Integrity is also required for the health of the people. A nation or a society in which truth cannot be assumed cannot long endure.

The basic issue in this Commandment is the integrity of one's word when spoken in the name of the Lord: the people of Israel were a covenanted people at Sinai. God had chosen them to be his witnesses. Through this people was to come a light to lighten the Gentiles. They were called to be a holy nation, a royal priesthood; and they had been signed with the mark of Yahweh. Before the face of all of the people of the earth, they were to be the bearers of the name of their God; so every act, every word, every thought of a member of the covenanted people was a reflection of the God whose people they were. The third Commandment covered all of their life, for it covered all of their word, their honor, their integrity, their truthfulness. From the smaller specific area of an oath taken in the name of the Lord, it spread to cover every transaction of every person who was a member of the covenant nation.

Christianity took over this concept: Christians conceived of themselves as the people of the New Covenant or the New Testament. The way one entered into this New Covenant was through the act of baptism. It is not an accident that at baptism you receive a name by which you are known, and you receive that name by being baptized in another name, the name of God, now called by Christians not Yahweh but Trinity, Father, Son, and Holy Spirit. It is with that name that you are marked at your baptism. The symbol of that name, the sign of the cross, is placed upon your forehead. This is the Christian Church's, the New Covenant's, way of saying, "The name of Christ thus becomes part of your identification. From your baptism on, everything you do, everything you say, everything you think is a reflection upon the name you wear." It is an all-encompassing concept, as indeed the biblical story is. Once more it makes almost ridiculous the sentimental claim of certain segments of our world that religion is a narrow area of life to which clergy ought to confine their attention, leaving the rest of the world to go by.

"You shall not take the name of the Lord your God in vain" expands even more inside the Christian revelation. Jesus, our Christ, says that the word of the Christian ought to be simply yea or nay, nothing more. Nothing more should ever be required of one who bears that name, no oath, no swearing by God or by holiness or by heaven above or by the earth beneath. For the word of a disciple of Jesus must always express the integrity that befits the name of Christ which that disciple bears. That is where the third Commandment touches your life and mine.

That may seem rather simple in our complex world. It may

be rather old-fashioned, and some may consider it out of style, but that is nonetheless the claim of the Christian Lord upon you and me. That is the Christian position to which we are bound by our baptism.

Finally, the name of God and consequently this Commandment did get involved in a very secondary way with the human phenomenon of profanity. There are some implications here that are important to understand. I suspect that I am less than objective in this area, for here again I cannot escape my early training in my rigidly moralistic home, where the attitudes were shaped and formed by my very bluestocking Presbyterian mother. I suspect that this training was more evident in the area of profanity than in any other area. I can remember being punished as a child for saying such profane words as *gosh* and *darn*. I never have liked the taste of Life-buoy! I don't suppose I used my first *hell* or *damn* until I was fully grown, and I must confess that I still wince—something inside me is triggered—when I hear the holy name of God said in an oath. *Goddamn* is an expression that offends me even today. And *Jesus Christ* shouted as an expletive always hits a jarring note in my emotions. I am not certain whether I can attribute this reaction only to my early training which created emotional tapes still in my head, ready to play whenever certain buttons are pushed. Beyond that training there is, I believe, an objective response. The names *God, Jesus,* and the *Christ* represent the holiest realities my life knows; and hence the profane use of these holy words, to me, constitutes an insensitive offense.

I have tried to analyze profanity, and I must say that it means different things to different people. For some people, profanity trips off their lips with such ease and with so little meaning that it is clearly of little significance to them. For still others, it is the only legitimate vocabulary of anger, and nothing else quite serves the purpose. For still others, and I guess that I am one of them, it almost constitutes blasphemy. I find it interesting that most of our oaths and our obscenities have either a religious or a sexual content. Sometimes the sexual content is a bit retarded and centers on certain body functions. It is interesting to me that the most intimate human experiences, namely the object of our worship and the object of human love, provide the vocabulary of profanity.

Look for just a moment at the religious symbols used in profanity, for these symbols have come to be viewed as covered by the third Commandment: "You shall not take the name of the Lord your God in vain." What are we really saying when we say "goddamn" or "Go to hell"? Both indicate, if we literalize them, that we have usurped the place of God and that we are in a position to decide what another's eternal destiny is to be, based upon our assessment of exactly what another is worth. That is really not profanity so much as it is blasphemy. I have taken the place of God when I can assign you to hell.

The expression "for Christ's sake" assumes that I am on the side of the angels, and unless you act out my will, you must be doing wrong. So "for Christ's sake" get with it and be like me. My sake and Christ's sake have become identical, and that is nothing less than self-idolatry.

Even the mild oaths, "gosh," "my goodness," "merciful father," all are forms of "my God." The word "gee" is nothing except shorthand for "Jesus." Even the phrase "for crying out loud" originally was a reference to Jesus on the cross.

Profanity ultimately expresses a kind of bankruptcy of language, for our profane symbols lose their meaning in very loose context. For example, I have heard people called "stupid as hell" and "smart as hell." You cannot be both! I have heard things described as "big as hell" and "little as hell." The weather is called "hot as hell" and "cold as hell," and the symbol really is violated there. Language that loose and that imprecise is, frankly, dumb as hell!

Sometimes, when the symbol is literalized it has a startling effect. A story is told about a man in a bar who looked up and saw a fellow drinker who seemed familiar. "Where in hell have I seen you before?" he inquired. To which the stranger responded, "I don't know. What part of hell do you come from?"

I suppose profanity has some therapeutic value. We get a great deal of emotion, hostility, and anger out with our expletives, and probably it is better to express these feelings verbally than physically. I suppose that it is inevitable that the most intimate human experiences, such as worship and sex, will supply the basic content for our oaths. I recall one occasion when I was playing tennis in Lynchburg, Virginia. My partner's wife missed a shot. She stopped and hit her racquet on the ground and shouted "Richard Nixon!" I thought that a rather innovative kind of profanity.

On other occasions in Lynchburg, I played a good deal of squash with an orthopedic surgeon. He was a violent man who looked something like a gorilla. He was huge, hairy, and given to the fullest possible expression of verbal abuse. He knew absolutely no finesse in life or on the squash court. In squash he only wanted to hit that ball as hard as he could, and when he missed a shot, he would hurl an oath out that you could hear a city block away. All of his oaths began with "Goddamn!" About midway through a match that I was playing with him, I stopped the game and said, "Bob, how about swearing at your profession instead of mine for a while. Next time you miss a shot, instead of taking it out on God, scream 'I hate aspirin.' " He agreed to try. A minute later, when his ball hit the tin, he shouted. "Goddamn it, I hate aspirin!" It was a partial victory.

Profanity is not an important area of human behavior. We all have different feelings about it. The real substance of this Commandment, the whole area of perjury, the truth, the integrity, the validity of one's word—that is important, for the very matrix of society is built upon the assumption that a man's word is good and truth can be expected in human interchange. That is as important as any other moral injunction to which the Commandments address themselves.

7

The Sabbath– The Meaning of Time

"R emember the Sabbath Day to keep it holy"—this is Commandment number four. I think it is essential that the biblical setting of these words be kept in mind. The scene is still Sinai, and the Hebrew people are encamped at the foot of the mountain. It is the moment of Covenant.

God, Yahweh, who had acted in history to bring this people out of slavery in Egypt, was now going to bind this people to himself and in the Covenant to make Israel a holy nation, a royal priesthood. Upon the twin themes of Exodus and Sinai the whole Book of Exodus turns. There is first the grace of the redemption that was Exodus, followed by the law of God's command that was Sinai. The selection by God of this people —Exodus—was followed by a call to obedience—Sinai. Exodus is always followed by Sinai. Grace is always followed by law. You are loved, then you respond with obedience. Love must always be accompanied by duty and discipline or it dissipates into a thin, vapid nothing.

It is in this setting and context that Israel hears what Yahweh, the God who has chosen them, now requires of them. The Ten Words sound like the tolling of a bell, vibrating into every corner of human life. They have stood the test of time.

Commandment number one: I am Yahweh. Simply the proclamation of God's being. I am, so you must respond.

Commandment number two: I am exclusive. You shall have no other gods. You shall make no images. You shall allow no loyalties that usurp my place. No other loyalty can be primary, not to a loved one, a clan, a nation, a church, not even to a creed. God is exclusive—radically exclusive.

Commandment number three: My name is holy. You who bear my name must not defile this name by being false with one another. Your word as my people is always spoken in my name. When you violate your word you take my name in vain.

Now we arrive at Commandment number four: the Sabbath is holy—you must remember it and you must observe it.

As we begin to explore this Commandment I hope you will put from your mind all of your previous connotations. For the Sabbath, like the subjects of the other Commandments, has had a long history of development. It has reflected the traditions of many ages and because of that, the substance and the profundity of what the Sabbath originally meant to the Jews is ofttimes lost.

I would like to get into this Commandment by starting not with its origins and coming forward, as we have done with the others, but rather by starting with its present traditions and corruptions and working backward to its origins, peeling off the layers in the process.

In the home in which I was raised the word "Sabbath" was applied to Sunday. That was a distortion, but that was my family's tradition. Sunday was to me the most unpleasant day in the entire week. It seemed to me that all the forces converged on me that day in a conspiracy to keep me from being a normal little boy. I had to wear special clothes—not school clothes or play clothes, but Sunday clothes—fancy, stiff, restrictive clothes that I dared not get dirty or torn. In these special clothes I was taken to Sunday school by my mother, who herself seldom went. My father never went.

Sunday school and church got communicated to me as something that kids had to do and naturally I looked forward to growing up so I too could do what I pleased on Sunday morning like my father and my mother.

Sunday school was a chore for me. I am in the ordained ministry in spite of my Sunday school training and not because of it. The thing I enjoyed most was getting my perfect attendance medal. I remember one or two of my teachers, but I can honestly say that I remember very little else.

Even though we did not stay for church and normally got home about 11 o'clock, still Sunday did not improve for me. I could not change my clothes and I could not get my clothes dirty. I hated those clothes. It was very difficult for me in that restrictive binding ever to break the Sabbath. I could not play marbles; I could not play tag or baseball; I could not even play roll-a-bat. As I looked around with my childish eyes, the adults who were in my world seemed to be doing the things that they wanted to do; only the kids seemed prohibited on the Sabbath. Maybe only kids have to keep the Sabbath I thought. Maybe Sabbath is like an allergy that can be outgrown in time. Movies were out. Games, especially card games, were the work of the devil. Television was not yet invented. Watching the Charlotte Hornets in the old Class B Piedmont League play baseball was making others work and thereby breaking the Sabbath, or so I was told. On occasion I would disobey and sneak out to Griffith Park in Charlotte to see the game anyway. I was usually caught, but if it was a doubleheader I considered it a worthwhile risk.

Sunday dragged on like eternity for me, boring me beyond endurance. I could visit relatives and I could read. I was strongly encouraged to read the Bible but those thin little golden-edged pages would constantly stick together or bend or tear. They seemed never to turn for my little fingers. And the language of that book, with the "thees" and "thous" and "asketh" and "beggeth," was to me incomprehensible at best and silly at worst. I am positive that part of my negativity toward the King James Bible was born on those Sunday afternoons.

Besides, I really did not like God. To me God was a stern heavenly father who spent his time telling you what you could not do or punishing you if you ever did it. I was convinced that God had never been a boy. He did not know what fun was. He never smiled beneath his long beard. I knew this because one day I asked my mother why Sundays were so different, so dull and boring. "Well, dear," my mother responded, "Sunday is the Lord's day." Well, in my mind anyone who had a day like that just could not be very nice.

Of course, I could not admit that, for I had had a healthy dose of the fear of God instilled in me by my mother. I grew up forced to do the religious thing and hating every minute of it. My weekends were ruined because Sunday was a part of every weekend. Imagine my delight and my surprise when I discovered that there is not one biblical injunction anywhere in any of the sixty-six books of Holy Scripture that prohibits working on Sunday—not one. For you see, Sabbath and Sunday are not the same. They never have been the same.

The Sabbath was the Jewish day of rest and was identified late in Hebrew history with the creation story in which God rested on the seventh day. But Sunday was never the seventh day, the day of rest.

Sunday was the Christian day of resurrection. It was the day on which God acted and it was the first day of the week, not the last. Sunday was originally, as a Christian holy day, marked not by withdrawal and rest but by celebration, festivity, and parties. The Holy Communion service, which very quickly became the service of worship designed for Christian people on the holy day, took on the original festive character of that Sunday. That is why that service was and is called a "celebration" of Holy Communion.

Early in Christian history both the Jewish Sabbath—the day of rest and the last day of the week—and the Christian Sunday —the day of celebration and the first day of the week—existed side by side. Early Christians observed both and the two were never confused. Sabbath had its emphasis on rest and Sunday its emphasis on festivity. But as Christianity moved away from its Jewish roots and into the Gentile world, the Sabbath day of rest faded and only the Sunday of celebration remained. For the first 1500 years of Christian history, Sunday's festive, celebrative nature was affirmed in Christendom.

Then along came John Calvin. John Calvin must have been exactly like my childhood image of God. Stern, long-faced, somber, boring, rigid, and no fun. He was undoubtedly one of the great minds of Christian history, but never one of my favorite theologians. His personality was that of a man who sucked sour persimmons for a hobby or who was constantly bothered by indigestion and gas pains. This man seemed to me to love rigid legalistic rules and regulations. He, more than anyone else in Christian history, dug back very deep into the Old Testament Sabbath day tradition with all of its restrictions, its admonitions to rest, and, taking them out of the

Jewish tradition, he dropped them down on the Christian Sunday. In the process he merged the two days and transformed the character of the Christian Sunday into that of the Jewish Sabbath in the most legalistic way. It was not the biblical Sunday but rather it was John Calvin's creation that I experienced on the first day of each week as a child. John Calvin's Sunday: rest from your labor; no fun today; church is a somber experience where if you laugh you must be sinful, where worshipers act as though they have lost their last friend; be quiet; this is God's house; stiff clothes; no marbles; no Charlotte Hornets. John Calvin's creation. None of that was originally part of the day of the resurrection.

What joy to discover that this kind of Sunday was rooted in John Calvin, not in the Bible, not in the Christian faith, not in the early tradition. Thus the first layer of tradition, the first layer of corruption and distortion of the concept of the Sabbath, is peeled back from this Commandment. The Christian Sunday is not the Jewish Sabbath and need not be observed by withdrawal from life or by refraining from raking your leaves or cutting your grass.

Some time ago, I was mowing my backyard on a Sunday afternoon when one of my neighbors, obviously a Calvinist, walked out of her house and spoke to me. I turned off the lawnmower to hear what she was saying. I should have left it on.

"You'd better be careful," she admonished. "I knew a minister several years ago who was cutting his grass on Sunday and he had a heart attack and died."

I smiled and allowed as how I had always heard that the good die young and I was sure she would live to a ripe old age.

Having separated the Christian Sunday from the Jewish Sabbath, we still need to explore the meaning of the Jewish Sabbath. Literally, in the Exodus account, it was identified with the seventh day of the week and tied in with the story of the creation. The seven-day story consumes Genesis One and the first four verses of Genesis Two. This is the second layer to which we must go. We know from our critical analysis of the Bible that the seven-day creation story of Genesis 1:1–2:4 is from the pen of the Priestly writer which is the last strand of Old Testament material to achieve written form. The Ten Commandments, as we have them in the Book of Exodus, are from the Elohist document, antedating the Priestly writer by at least two hundred years, but the Elohist account of the Ten Commandments has clearly been edited by the Priestly writer. There is doubt that a Sabbath tradition in Hebrew history was originally tied in with the story of the creation. Rather it seems that the Sabbath day rest injunction was added by the Priestly writer many years after the simple Commandment "Remember the Sabbath and keep it holy" became a part of the Jewish consensus of the Ten Words. It is only in the editorial expansion of the Priestly writer that the Sabbath tradition is identified with the creation story.

In the version of the Ten Commandments given in Deuteronomy, for example, the Sabbath is identified not with the creation, but with the Exodus, and this version is perhaps 150 years older than the Priestly tradition. The Deuteronomic writer enjoins the Sabbath day of rest upon Israel and upon every life that the people of Israel touch, both fellow Israelites and slaves, both human beings and beasts of burden, because, says Deuteronomy, rest is essential to life. Human beings of every station and even animals must not be exploited. Do not forget, says the Book of Deuteronomy, that you were slaves, victims of exploitation in Egypt. Do not fail to recognize that periodic rest from labor is a right of every human being and every living thing. It is not a privilege that one generously bestows. It is a right guaranteed by God. Thus we uncover a second layer of tradition on the Sabbath.

If we drive the Sabbath back even deeper into Hebrew history, it appears not to have been originally associated with a day of the week at all, but with a celebration of the new moon. It was originally a monthly festival. It was a time when the whole tribe required a change of pace, a time of withdrawal and rest. The word *Sabbath* comes from the Hebrew verb form that meant "to rest." The Sabbath grew into a weekly festival, anthropologists suspect, because of the influence first from the Sumerians and later from the Babylonians. It was the means by which the Hebrews reminded themselves of the holiness of time, all time. On the Sabbath the Hebrew people deliberately and self-consciously, in the words of the old hymn, "took time to be holy." Sabbath thus originally gave their life a rhythm, a self-conscious quality of worship. That was its origin and from that it grew into its present shape, first moving from a monthly festival to a weekly festival, then becoming identified with the creation story, and finally being laden with injunctions of very rigid forms of rest.

There is no doubt in my mind that the present Jewish observance of the Sabbath derives from the period of the Exile, not earlier, which we can date from 597 to 539 B.C.; and I believe that the present Jewish observance of the Sabbath is the creation of the Priestly writer. The Sabbath met very specific needs in the Exile community, needs for self-identification, survival, and so on. The Exile community had been ripped from their native soil, torn away from their sacred tradition, separated from their temple, their worship, their homeland. They were prisoners of war. The deepest threat they faced was the threat of assimilation, losing themselves in the dominant culture of Babylon. It was under the leadership of men like Ezekiel and the exiled Temple priesthood that two customs were resurrected and made the very marks of Judaism. One was circumcision and the other was a rigidly enforced observance of the Sabbath day, a weekly ritual. The seven-day creation story was written at that very late date to undergird this new emphasis. It was written to help the Sabbath achieve this new status. The Jews observed the Sabbath and then created the seven-day creation story to give it a theological basis in its origins.

The two customs, circumcision and Sabbath observance, made the Judaism of the Jews obvious. On the body of every Jewish male was the sign of his Judaism, and every seventh day every Jew became publicly discernible, for he or she engaged in no commerce and did no labor. Under pressure from the Jewish leadership, then, this restrictive attitude, this benchmark of Judaism, was defined and redefined. Thirty-nine different kinds of work were specifically prohibited. No medical attention for chronic or nonemergency situations was allowed. In the New Testament recall how Jesus was castigated by the authorities of the Jewish priesthood for healing the man with the withered hand on the Sabbath. A withered hand is a chronic, not an emergency situation, and therefore when Jesus healed the man with the withered hand he broke the Sabbath. Broken bones could not be set on the Sabbath for, even though it might be painful, a broken bone in the arm or leg would not normally be the cause of death.

There was also no embalming of the dead on the Sabbath. This too is apparent from the life of Jesus. He was taken from his cross on Friday so his friends could avoid defiling the Sabbath, which begins at sundown on Friday. There was no time to embalm. Jesus was wrapped in a linen shroud and placed in the tomb. The sole reason that the women came to the tomb at dawn on the first day of the week bearing spices was to do the work of embalming, for this was the first moment beyond the Sabbath that this work could be done.

One could only walk three-fifths of a mile on the Sabbath. Any more walking was considered a violation of the injunction to refrain from work. Three-fifths of a mile was the distance a priest had to walk to do his priestly duties in the Temple on the Sabbath day. The Book of Acts refers to the Mount of Olives as a Sabbath day's journey from Jerusalem, that is, three-fifths of a mile.

Observance of the Sabbath came to be the holiest liturgical practice in all of Judaism. But please understand, every liturgical practice grows out of a deep perception of human need. This Commandment ultimately has to do with the necessity for worship. It demands that the human spirit put away routines and take time to relate to that which creates its life, that which undergirds its being.

I believe a case can be made for the activity of worship as that which finally separates humanity from lower animals. I believe that life is holy, all of life—plants, animals, human beings. Life is that throbbing, beating, growing, expanding reality that binds both the simplest and the most complex organisms into a common experience. All living things share in the deepest, holiest power of the universe, the power of life itself, which is mysterious and wondrous, intriguing and divine. Yet human life is more. Human life has evolved to a stage of development that enables the human being to commune with the source of life, to stand in awe of it, to feel both alienated or out of touch with it, and in communion with it, and that is worship. Worship requires time. It requires self-conscious practice. It was this that the Sabbath was originally designed to provide in the life of the Hebrew people.

The Sabbath was institutionalized in Judaism to enable this quality of rest and communion with the divine to become obvious, real, and a part of Jewish life. When the Jews finally settled on a seven-day week ending in the Sabbath to make people self-conscious about the rhythm of life, they numbered the other days with reference to the Sabbath. So Monday was the second day after Sabbath, Thursday was the fifth day after the Sabbath, and so on. Then once the Sabbath, with its human yearning and its sense of communion with the ulti-mate, was defined, once it became the liturgical center of life, then the tradition of how it was to be observed developed. Finally the observance distorted the meaning, and rigidity set in. The Sabbath of my youth, thus, became obvious and appar-ent, but the Sabbath of my youth is not the Sabbath of God. When we look deeply enough we discover that every people needs a Sabbath, a day of withdrawal from life's normal rou-tines, a day to contemplate the holy self-consciously. I cannot support blue laws on the basis of some supposed biblical in-junction against working on Sunday, for there is no such in-junction. I am thus a cause of despair to certain local lawmak-ers and certain fundamentalist clergy. But I can support blue laws on a psychological and a spiritual basis. People need the rhythm of work and rest, and people need a time set aside for worship and for searching within for life's holiest dimension. It is that element of the Jewish Sabbath which is and must be a part of the Christian Sunday, and this is essential, I believe, for the emotional health and well-being of human life and for our spiritual maturity.

The Jews understood that rest and withdrawal were rights guaranteed to all of life by their creator, hence, these were written into their holy Law. These were not privileges ac-quired but rights which could not be abrogated. In their ob-servance is a clue to the meaning of life.

Finally, the worship that is focused on the Sabbath for Jews and on Sunday for Christians is an attempt to open our eyes to see the holiness of all time. Sabbath in its ultimate sense is not so much a day as an attitude. Jews on Saturday, Christians on Sunday, all celebrate self-consciously in worship the holiness of God in every moment of life. We cannot make life holy until we, by living, become people who are aware of the source of life. We cannot make love real unless we, by loving, reveal ourselves to be in touch with the source of love. We cannot participate in resurrection unless we do so by our caring, our giving, and our sharing in the act of making all life and all time new. That is what lies behind Sabbath.

All life and all time are experienced as holy. Every experience is a way through which God can be perceived. Our need is to take time to develop eyes that can perceive and hearts that can respond to this understanding of life and worship. This is the ultimate meaning of Sabbath. It is also the ultimate meaning of Sunday. Here and here alone they are one.

Remember then, we are commanded, "Keep holy the Sabbath of God."

8

The Meaning of Parenthood

The fifth Commandment states "Honor your father and your mother, that your days may be long in the land the Lord your God gives you." This is the first commandment that specifically moves beyond our duty toward God and focuses on our duty toward our neighbor. Appropriately enough, that duty begins with the intimate relationship between children and their parents.

Note that this is the only one of the Commandments governing our duty toward our neighbor that is expressed in a positive way. All of the others place restraints and curbs upon our behavior. "You shall not kill." "You shall not commit adultery." "You shall not steal." This Commandment, however, calls us to act out a positive attitude.

I begin our consideration of this Commandment in what might be a startling place. I do not believe that it is easy nor do I even believe that it is natural to love one's parents. I suspect that statement will surprise some of you because our culture works so hard to create a nostalgic, romantic idealization of both motherhood and fatherhood that will convince us that loving our parents is a virtue we all must exemplify. I suppose that there is nothing I desire more deeply in life than to know that I have the love and respect of my three daughters.

But consider the data. First look at the animal world. We human beings are biologically a part of the animal world, hence it should not surprise us to discover that some of the patterns of animal behavior appear in our behavior. In the animal world, the sole function of parents is to conceive, give birth, nurture, and wean. Once the animal is weaned, few species continue any relationship with parents, or even notice or know that there was ever anything special about the parental relationship. In the animal world there is no parent-child dependency in the full-grown animal. There is no parent-child relationship that survives the weaning experience.

So the human response to parents, mixed as it is with duty, guilt, and emotional dependency, appears not to arise out of any biological necessity. It appears to be an unnatural phenomenon in animal nature. There is nothing in the animal world resembling what we call the maternal instinct, for example, that survives weaning. Thus, the response of the adult human to his or her parent appears to be an acquired behavioral characteristic of civilization.

Second, when one turns to anthropological study of primitive cultures, one discovers a somewhat startling revelation; namely that the economic factor of life more than any other factor has dictated the ethical behavior norms, particularly those norms which relate to the various generations. The economic factors of life in many primitive cultures dictated that those members of the tribe who could not share the burden of the struggle for survival were not carried by the tribe, even as revered, elderly dependents of the society. If a person was strong enough to survive to an old age, which, in fact, was very rare in primitive societies, he or she was often treated shamefully with no qualms of conscience. The elderly in many cultures were banished from the tribe, left to starve, or even worse.

It did not seem in those societies of human beings that there was a reverence for age or even a devotion to those who were one's physical parents. These characteristics appear to be learned rather than instinctual. Certainly they are not universal or normative responses in primitive life.

Add to this the insight of the psychological disciplines, which have confirmed many of the truths expressed in ancient mythology, the truths of rivalry and overt hostility that mark the parent-child relationship, particularly when the child reaches maturity. We begin to suspect that the romantic love and respect that we are told mark motherhood and fatherhood are in fact nothing more than a thin veneer of civilization that covers intense human emotions. For in the psychological maturation process, the role of the child is finally to replace the parent. That means they are rivals, which creates guilt in the child as he has to take over the responsibility and, in fact, destroy the power of the parent. From the parent's point of view, the child is always the successor and no one likes having his successor around, for that carries with it what Paul Tillich called the threat of non-being. This means that the parent's destiny is to lose power and status, and to sacrifice position. This creates fear and hostility in the parent. These raw emotions are a part of life but we do not like to discuss them. Yet we are all aware of the Oedipal conflicts and complexes, named after the ancient Greek myth of Oedipus, the king who fell in love with his mother after killing his father. Freud has made us aware that every child goes through an Oedipal experience, once more laying bare emotions that most of us are uncomfortable with and many are not willing to face.

Yet we are aware that a significant number of the murders committed in this country are committed within family relationships. They do not grow out of motherly love.

As a counselor and pastor, I have seen people in my office gripping the chair until you could see the whites of their knuckles while they told me how much they loved their fathers. One begins to read body language far more than words. As a counselor I am intensely aware of hostile jealousy that flows between mother and daughter and is particularly intensified when the mother begins to reach the psychologically burdensome menopause years just as the daughter blooms into the fullness of her feminine form. A similar hostility marks the father-son relationship as the father's physical power wanes and the son overtakes him. The first time the son beats the father in golf is a celebrated family event. Indeed, if you look deeply enough under the romantic, nostalgic sentimentality that surrounds the culture's celebration of motherhood and fatherhood, you find something quite different from love and devotion. Examine the references to mother in profanity, for example. A "son of a what" do we call one another? A "mother what" do we call one another? See what our profanity says about our underlying, hidden emotions?

I am personally convinced that sentimentality is almost always a cover for unacceptable hostility that we are not willing to face. Nothing is more sentimental than our culture's celebration of Mother's Day or Father's Day. The great devotion to parents that is couched in poetry and song is to me nothing but an effort to cover a deep and abiding antipathy between the generations. For example, when a man "gives up his life to care for his mother" one may look for something more than love going on. There is an emotional dependency that breeds hostility. Possessive mothers produce dependent sons who dutifully care for their mothers while they deal inwardly and usually unconsciously with great amounts of hostility. No one finally loves the person upon whom he or she is dependent and some way, even if a socially acceptable way, will always be found to let that hostility out.

Listen to the emotional place accorded mother in country and western music. Mother is sung about with the same kind of deep, touching emotions that embrace God and Old Shep. But have you ever noticed that most country and western songs about mother are about the death of mother? I am suggesting that the relationship between the grown child and the parent is not a simple, romantic, nostalgic, sentimental relationship. It is a relationship of conflict and tension that needs to be resolved or, at the very least, faced. It is a relationship of love and hate, of dependency and rebellion, of displacement and identification. When you get underneath the sentimentality that surrounds the cultural image of motherhood and fatherhood, you have touched one of the deepest guilt-producing emotions of human life. The Hebrew people, in their incredible insight and genius in understanding human life, seemed to understand this, and so into their most sacred Ten Words from God they have enjoined us in the name of God to rise above the inner conflicts and give honor to those who have given us the gift of life.

Notice there is no Commandment requiring parents to love and care for their children. There is no children's day celebrated on the calendar. Most species of animal life provide basic life-giving nurture to the offspring. The fifth Commandment assumes, accurately I believe, that the honoring of the parents is a calling to a higher way than the instinctual, natural behavior patterns would produce. Otherwise we would not work so hard to create the sentimentality to keep parents safe from the natural instincts of rejection and displacement.

Some people will reject this as nonsense. Some will get angry at the very idea because the revelation of this level of life is unpleasant. You may feel compelled to assert that your parents were close to gods or at least close to angels, but that is because most of us cannot face the unconscious levels of our own inner conflict and our own inner hostility. When I say these things in lectures I never fail to notice a nervous restlessness that marks the audience. These are feelings most of us would prefer to ignore yet it is obvious that they are not only real but deep in the very heart of our life. In a non-neurotic form, these emotions are expressed in adolescent rebellion that, I hope, we all went through. A teenager suddenly decides that his or her parents do not know anything about anything, that they are probably the two dumbest adults in the world; but by the time the teenager gets to be twenty-one or so, it is amazing how much his or her parents were able to learn in so short a time. This comes out of a natural conflict and that is healthy.

Not everyone, however, has a healthy adjustment to these emotions, and in a more neurotic person, the hostility can become strange and destructive. I hope you will pardon this reference but it is a natural quotation and it is rather revealing. I heard a psychiatrist once define psychoanalysis as a process which you undergo to enable you to say "son of a bitch" in front of your m-o-t-h-e-r. I have never heard a better definition. I have even known one wildly neurotic young adult who entered a hospital and had plastic surgery done on his navel so he could remove the last vestige of evidence that he ever had a relationship with his mother. These attitudes reveal that beneath the external level of the parent-child relationship, there are deep and volatile human emotions that govern that relationship. Loving or honoring one's parents is not a simple matter. Once more the Ten Commandments sink beneath the obvious and probe the deepest inner recesses of human life. Once more the Commandments call us to live out a higher destiny, a higher humanity that befits the elected people of

God, whose lives have been so touched by grace and love that they can overcome the conflicts present in their own inner lives and give honor to their fathers and mothers. The primary focus of this Commandment, contrary to what most people think, is on adult parental relationships, not parent-child relationships. The Commandment aims chiefly at the relationship between a grown adult and an elderly parent. It was never intended to be a club enabling parents to control their children by quoting this Commandment to them to modify the child's behavior. This Commandment is not an injunction for children to obey. It does not force children to honor that which is not honorable. It does not bless parental brutality or child abuse. It does not require submission to or toleration of unacceptable behavior by parents toward children. Many people carry this kind of psychological burden, unable to express their negative feelings, unable to work them out, finding themselves under the burden of a law that says no matter what your real feelings are you are supposed to honor and love and obey your parents. That is not in this Commandment.

I recall some twenty-three years ago when, as a young seminarian serving a congregation of tenant farm families in rural Virginia, one of my duties was to teach a class for high school students each Sunday morning. These children and teenagers were not well-educated or sophisticated. They were simple, earthy people. My subject was the Ten Commandments. When we got to this Commandment, "Honor your father and your mother," I became aware of the agitation of one lovely blond girl, about fourteen, who was in the first blush of adult feminine beauty. That beauty, however, was marred by an ugly scar across her forehead. I knew the source of that scar. Some years earlier her father had come home drunk and abusive one Saturday night and had kicked this child down the stairs, splitting her head open. The family did not seek medical attention. Perhaps they were too ignorant or too poor or too afraid of questions being asked. So the forehead was left to heal as best it could, with home remedies probably exaggerating the disfigurement.

Must the Christian Church in the name of morality lay upon this child the duty to accept that abuse and still honor her father? I think not. That is to focus this Commandment on the parent-child phase of life and to read it in terms of childlike respect and obedience. That is not its focus. This Commandment is a working principle designed to govern the obligation of adults to their elderly parents. It is not a command to obey or to tolerate abusive behavior. It is not directed to children. In the life of this little girl "father" was a word that conjured up feelings of fear and pain.

Please do not be simplistic or sentimental about this Commandment. We are to honor fatherhood and motherhood when those concepts are adequately expressed in human life, but beyond that there is no ethic of control in the fifth Commandment.

Consider another dimension of the parent-child relationship. Note that even in the paternalistic culture of ancient Israel, the Commandment includes both parents—both father and mother. We have lived in a male-dominated world for a very long time and that male dominance is expressed in the biblical literature. But despite these expressions of sexism, the Hebrews still knew enough about human life to be able to assert very specifically that humanity is not male or female. Humanity in its deepest, fullest form is only realized in the union of the two. I do not mean to say that the single adult—bachelor, maiden lady, divorced man or woman, widow or widower—is somehow less human. I do say that in creation the ideal for the fullness of human life is found in that union of the male and female toward which we are driven by our deep emotional need, driven by our intense physical desire, and driven by an inner sense of our incompleteness. These things mark all of life, and beyond that each of us needs to be the recipient of both feminine love and masculine love in order to achieve our full individual maturity and humanity. That is, not only is humanity best achieved in the union of a man and a woman, but also two parents, one male and one female, are essential to the full growth and development of every individual, healthy human life. When for reasons of human frailty or tragic sickness and premature death the love of one or the other of the parents is lost, there is in the life of the offspring a tremendous need for compensation.

My own father died when I was twelve, and though I did not know it at the time, I spent most of my teenage years looking for a father substitute. I found one and he happened to be a priest of the Church. He determined perhaps as much as anyone I could name the entire shape of my life.

It is very difficult in this age of new sensitivity to sexual discrimination to talk about the characteristics of feminine love and masculine love, for there is no assurance that you are accurately discerning a biological reality or a cultural role. But we can at least analyze the kinds of love that are needed by every child, and we can see the ways that the culture has organized to meet those needs, needs which, when driven deeply enough, necessitate the wisdom and the sanctity of a monogamous marriage and a faithful living together as far as possible so that the full work of parenting can be done.

Apparently our humanity requires two distinct emotional realities.* First every one of us needs the security to be. We need love that is not discriminating, love that loves us just because we are, not because we do. We need a sense of belonging, a community, an identity that no one can take away from us. We tend to get these qualities in the kind of love that normally derives from the feminine figure, the mother image. A mother loves her baby in anticipation. Her love is graceful love that is based on the baby's being, not on the baby's doing. Her love is given without distinction, not given for achievements but simply because the baby is. It is indissoluble. Nothing can destroy the bond of love. In order to be human we must build upon this security of being, this sense of belonging, this grace of acceptance. This is the first layer, the bedrock of the human experience.

But security alone does not produce humanity. Love that loves us because we are, love which is unchallenged or unsupplemented results finally not in full life but in a twisted, sick dependency. For the fullness of humanity there must be a second principle, a counter principle which I tend to identify with the father figure in the psychological development of the

*Much of the following discussion is based on *The Art of Loving* by Dr. Erich Fromm (New York: Harper & Row, 1956).

human being. This second principle I call the "drive to become." The security to be must be coupled with the drive to become in order to achieve full humanity. The drive to become is received in the kind of love that sets standards. It is the challenge to accomplish, it is the discrimination of judgment, the reward for excellence. Love that creates the drive to become by definition is not love that is equally shared. It is given to the one who best deserves it. It is not based on being, but on doing. This kind of love alone is also inadequate. The drive to become without the security to be would finally create not humanity but a jungle where might makes right, where the capacity to rule is the reward bestowed upon the superachiever, and unchallenged it would finally produce not humanity, but a sick tyranny. Full, true humanity is the perfect and absolute balance betwen the security to be, which I identify with mother love, and the drive to become, which I identify with father love. Both are essential to our humanity and the sources of our humanity.

These qualities have been understood in our concepts of God. In the history of Western civilization at least, God is masculine. He is referred to as "Father." He is pictured as a judge. He is seen as the dispenser of rewards and punishments that we call heaven and hell. He is portrayed as the distant giver of rules and commandments which set standards and drive us to become. But this Father God has never existed alone. He is always seen working through the Church which, interestingly, is called "Mother Church." To this divine mother we belong equally at our baptism, not based on our doing, but on our being, and in the bosom of this mother we are nurtured, fed, loved, "just as we are without one plea." Here we are forgiven, accepted, and made secure to be, all of which enables us to be challenged by the Father God's will to become.

Parenthetically, I am convinced that the matter which really separates political conservatives and liberals is not an issue or a rational and well thought out attitude—one's political attitudes are hardly ever rational, that is why we get so emotional when we talk about them. One's political attitudes, I am beginning to believe, are rooted finally not in the issues, or in what is right or wrong, but in whether or not one's life is shaped primarily by the masculine drive to become or the feminine security to be.

The masculine drive to become is expressed politically by an attitude that says everyone gets what he or she deserves and nothing more. Those who are thus motivated are against welfare systems and governmental social security systems. They are much more individualistic, opposed to all forms of collectivization. These are the conservative principles. On the other hand, the feminine security to be is expressed politically by an attitude that says everyone should be treated equally, that everyone should be cared for by the superparent, the government, from the cradle to the grave with all kinds of security programs from Aid to Dependent Children to Medicare. This attitude always drives toward a collectivization aimed at caring for all according to their needs alone. And these are liberal principles.

Lest you think this is too far-fetched, let me point out that when the drive to become is unchallenged it becomes in the political arena a right-wing fascism which is bound to have master race manifestations. This political point of view appeared in its most blatant form in Western civilization in a country known to its people as the *"Father*land." The security to be, when unchallenged, becomes in the political arena a left-wing communal state which in its purest form would take from each what they have to give and give to each according to their need. This political expression has appeared in its most blatant form in Western civilization in a country known to its people as *"Mother* Russia."

The maternal love, the security to be, and the paternal love, the drive to become, must, I believe, be kept together in perfect balance or humanity is destroyed. Every liberal needs a conservative to argue with and every conservative needs a liberal to challenge him. We are meant for each other and if the tension ever departs from life, our humanity is threatened.

Thus the fifth Commandment enjoins us to live as recipients of both the love of a mother and the love of a father. To preserve that pattern, this Commandment calls us to rise above our internal conflicts and emotions and to honor the meaning of fatherhood and the meaning of motherhood, that life may continue and that our days may be long in the land which the Lord our God has given us.

9

The Sacredness of Life

You shall not kill" is the sixth Commandment. It is crisp and clear, blunt and straightforward, unequivocal. Its meaning is not hidden, but as we begin to probe that meaning, even this Commandment opens up to a new and deeper understanding of life. Behind it lies an attitude toward life, a concept of creation, and a biblical insight into human nature.

Keep in mind that the Ten Commandments were originally given as part of God's word to the people of the Covenant— the people of Israel have been chosen as the redeemed. The people of Israel are the recipients of the grace of God and now the responsibilities of being the Covenant people are being spelled out. The Commandments are a part of God's call to live out the meaning of grace. Like great tolling bells they reverberate to every corner and crevice of life. They are not just rules but a call to rise above the natural instincts of our humanity, to achieve a level of nobility that befits the people of the Covenant. This is the context in which the Commandments must be heard and understood.

Human beings, contrary to our own propaganda, are not peaceful, nonviolent animals. We have evolved along with all of nature into our present existence. If Charles Darwin was correct, the evolutionary process was an intense struggle from which only the fittest survived. Survival was not by anything less than tooth and claw. The basic issues in that struggle were economic—that is, the basic struggle of human life was originally the economic struggle for food. Food was taken from the animal world first in the hunt (kill or be killed); then as civilization progressed, mankind got its food from domesticated herds. In the plant world food was chosen first from wild edible grains and fruits of nature, and then was systematically planted, cultivated, and harvested. In both methods, however, there was an intense competition. If their sources failed, groups of people would have to seize their food by force from other groups of human beings or else risk starving to death. To kill for food was a natural and normal part of life—even if it meant killing other human beings. Competition was the very essence of existence, and since the prize of competition was no less than life itself, the competition was often to the bitter end. The vanquished was the victim—and the emotions produced in this struggle for survival constitute a very basic aspect in what might be called human nature, although they are deeply submerged in our inner being.

We don't like to look this deeply into ourselves. We prefer to paper over the raw emotions that boil beneath the surface of our thin layer of civilization. We like to perfume the cesspools of violence that lurk beneath our conscious minds. We have adopted the saccharine attitudes required to get along in a complicated world, but none of this changes the fact that we human beings are prone to violence; we are jealous, competitive, and capable of hatred and killing. If this were not so the television screens would not be so filled with violence and death. Through television shows we live vicariously. We drain our emotions nightly before the tube. We portray our violence realistically via the evening news, or in fantasy through westerns, detective stories, and police chronicles. These things would not entertain us unless they made contact with something deep within our psyche—something civilization alone will never abrogate.

I do not believe it an accident that one of the earliest stories in the biblical narrative has to do with the act of killing. The murder occurs not between strangers but between brothers, whose names are Cain and Abel. The biblical mind very brilliantly probes human life, for brothers are consumed with a murderous hate. Once again we have to sink between the sentimentality that adorns the surface of life and face the deeper realities. In our sentimentalized civilization we love to talk about brotherly love. We even set aside a week each year to celebrate brotherhood. Note it is one week out of fifty-two.

One of our favorite phrases is "the brotherhood of man under the fatherhood of God." But look at life: how many of you have a brother and how well did you and your brother get along when you were growing up? Is brotherly love a reality or a civilized facade to cover an intense rivalry, jealousy, hostility?

Of course I loved my younger brother when I was a boy. I was constantly told I was supposed to, and so I said I did. But an awful lot of accidents happened to him whenever he was alone with me.

We were see-sawing once when we were quite young. I weighed more than he so I could keep his end high. I kept him there for so long on one occasion that he decided to jump off. It certainly wasn't my fault that he broke his arm. Little kids ought not to jump from high places.

I recall another occasion when we were having some repairs made on our home. A few pieces of sawed lumber were lying around on the ground. I picked up a piece that had been cut to a sharp angle and threw it up into the sky as high as I could throw it. Could I help it if my little brother just happened to run exactly into the spot where it came down? He has a lovely scar in the top of his head today as a memento of his carelessness. Little kids ought to watch where they are going.

There were lots of other experiences. I remember when I was twelve and he was nine: I decided it was his big brother's duty to teach him the manly art of self-defense. It was, of course, for his own good, I told him. We put on boxing gloves and under the guise of a socially acceptable sport I gave him a broken nose and a deviated septum. Of course I would not do that today for we are both adults and not only do I respect and admire him but also he is 6 feet 4 inches tall and weighs 210 pounds.

Brotherly love? I doubt if that will ever bring peace to the world—and somehow the Hebrews understood this. Long before Freud, they delved deeply into the human psyche and though they did not call it by this name they understood sibling rivalry. They wrote about it, even showing it leading to murder.

Every child who is born displaces the one immediately before him or her. No one likes to be displaced at any age.

Hostility flows when displacement occurs. Jealousy exists when displacement is achieved. Rivalry is intense. These are the forces that create sibling rivalry—and here the urge to kill is born.

How does the first child feel when the second child is born? The first child has no way of anticipating the arrival of the second. He never expected to share his center of attention. Then a "bundle of joy" arrives, taking mom away to the hospital for a few days and then making her much less attentive when she does return. Child number one feels exactly as a husband would feel if he arrived home after work one day and his wife greeted him by saying, "Come on into the bedroom dear, I want you to meet my second husband who's come to live with us! You must be sweet and love him and share everything with him." He is grabbed in the pit of his stomach by the knowledge that he can be replaced by the threat of nonbeing, and anger, envy, and hostility flow quickly, and the urge to kill is easy to understand.

Sibling rivalry exists all through life. It changes targets, but it never disappears. It is no wonder that civil wars are the bloodiest wars, for wars fought within the family always are.

Cain finally rises up and slays his brother Abel—expressing elemental human emotions. The emotions that caused that murder are in us, hidden deeply away but bubbling forth in explosions of temper, fits of passion, acts of prejudice, feelings of jealousy, desires to vindicate, needs to insult, to put down —ambition for power or status.

Civilization has repressed the murderous raw emotions of human life, but they are still present in every one of us, for they are part of our humanity. They are natural to the deeper recesses of our souls.

The Commandment "You shall not kill" speaks to this level of life. Its somber note reverberates into our innermost depths. The Commandment is not just a curb of civilization or one more means of repression. It is a call to a new creation, a new humanity. Remember that the Law according to the Book of Exodus is given to the people of the Covenant. It is to be the response of those who have been chosen, "redeemed," freed. It is a law given to those who are the elect—the loved ones.

The Hebrew verb "to kill" used in this verse of the Book of Exodus is spelled *rsh*. It appears in the Old Testament forty-six times. It is not easy to define. In some sense to render it "do not murder" rather than "do not kill" is more accurate, for it does not seem, originally at least, to have ruled out killing in a war or execution by the proper authorities for some serious crime against the community. Originally it probably forbade taking the law into one's own hands and prohibited an illegal killing which threatened the sanctity and the security of the community. It was limited to the tribe. It protected against violence so that the tribe could survive and a sense of tribe could be engendered. Yet no sooner is this aspect stated than its meaning begins to expand. In the Book of Numbers the same verb that appears in this Commandment is used to describe a legal execution. Thus all killing begins to be questioned.

Israel is never happy with any form of killing, legal or illegal. This people saw life as the gift of God. Very quickly the tradition of this people began to temper the Law. Cities of refuge were set up to protect one who had killed unintentionally. Here he could wait until his case could be heard, though he was still technically called a murderer. Before the eighth century B.C. other changes once more tempered this verb. At that time the injunction against killing was limited only to those acts of violence that arose from personal feelings of hatred and malice. The scope of the freedom to kill legally was being narrowed.

On the other end of the spectrum, by the time of the Priestly writer in the Book of Leviticus in the fifth century B.C., the injunction against murder had been expanded to include hating another in one's heart, even if one did not actually kill. Obviously, it is not a big step from there to Jesus' words in the Sermon on the Mount, "You have heard it said: You shall not kill. But I say do not hate—do not threaten, do not insult—for if you do, you have already murdered." The literalness of the Commandment thus fuzzes in both directions. It is not nearly so crisp as we imagine. You shall not kill is an abstract ideal but life and circumstances qualify it as happens to every Commandment.

In these tempering ways the Hebrew people began to act out an attitude toward life that was a direct result of their understanding of God. These things happened to this Commandment because of the Hebrew sense of God and worship.

God was the ultimate source of life. God was holy, therefore life itself had to be holy, all life, not just human life. The whole creation had to be responded to with reverence. God created this world. He looked upon it, he pronounced it good. Human life was created to preside over this world, to tend it, to love it, to enhance it as a good steward. To use the things of this world properly was an act of worship; to exploit the creation, to destroy the environment was an act of denying God.

The Hebrew creation legend proclaimed that life had come not just out of the soil but also from the animating, vitalizing breath of God. God breathed his *Nephesh* into Adam. Only because of this was Adam "a living soul."* So were all the children of Adam, whether good or bad, male or female, in bondage or free, members of the clan or aliens. The seeds of universalism are in the Hebrew attitude toward life, and this attitude is expressed in the sixth Commandment, "You shall not kill."

The Hebrews thus were quick to act against practices in the ancient world that were common to other people but which violated the principle of the sacredness of life. Infanticide was prohibited in the Old Testament. The abandonment of babies, especially female babies, was certainly not unusual even among the Romans. To the Roman writer Tacitus the Jewish prohibition against infanticide was a reason for anti-Semiticism.

On the other end of life's spectrum the Jews, because they held to the sacredness of life, refused to dispatch their elderly to a certain death.

This theme is crucial to the biblical story and central, I believe, to the increasing complexities of the twentieth century. Because life was holy to the Hebrews, killing in any form was increasingly questioned. Hence the emotions that fed the

---

*Soul is the King James word—"being" would be a better translation of the Hebrew.

anger that led to the act of murder came to be covered by this Commandment. So again the scope of the Commandment expanded.

The Commandment was interpreted to forbid suicide. Suicide is an expression of self-hatred so intense that it chops away at the holiness of life. The Hebrews did not understand the psychological dimensions of this as we do, but they did understand that it was a serious distortion of God's plan for each person, for that plan calls for the fullness of life. Situations will temper this too, so let us not be moralistic even about suicide. There are some circumstances where suicide seems to me to be an affirmation of life, not a denial. Listen to two episodes and decide. I know a man who committed suicide after he developed a particularly painful malignancy. All hope of cure was gone. To tolerate the pain would have required the addictive use of mind-altering drugs. He chose to die by his own hand while still in control of his faculties. Is that decision a denial of life or an enhancement of it?

In another instance a man overextended himself financially and was on the brink of financial ruin. The only thing that could save the security and the college education of his almost-grown children was an immediate infusion of capital. The banks refused to lend him any more money. He had only one other asset. He carried an immense amount of life insurance, so he "liquidated his final asset." He saved his family's financial security by committing suicide. Argue the pros and cons of that one someday. Was it a denial of life or not?

Neither is capital punishment a clear and simple issue. The Bible certainly decrees legal executions. One cannot use the Bible to support the abolition of capital punishment without twisting it badly. Before you leap with a kind of bloodthirsty glee and rush to reinstate the death penalty, however, read the Bible carefully. Death is prescribed as the punishment for a host of crimes including murder, treason, kidnapping, idolatry, blasphemy, false prophecy, witchcraft, breaking the Sabbath, rape, adultery, incest, perversion, uttering a curse, striking a parent, bearing false witness in a death penalty trial. Yet as soon as the decree was handed down, the Hebrew sense of the sacredness of life began to humanize the punishment, making the death penalty harder and harder to exact, just as we have done today.

If the accused confessed, death was forbidden. Death could not be exacted on circumstantial evidence alone; two witnesses had to agree that a murder was deliberate, that hatred was premeditated, that the killer was warned but did not heed the warning. Finally the witnesses had to be willing to carry out the execution personally.

In these ways the spirit of the Bible overcame the letter of the Law.

Let me state, for what it is worth, my firm conviction that the death penalty should not be revived for any reason in our nation today. A civilized society must deter criminal elements, but it does not need to seek revenge. Revenge does nothing except vent self-destructive hostility. There is no evidence that the death penalty deters capital crimes. If there is no evidence, then angry revenge must be recognized as the only motive for the death penalty, and that is beneath the behavior of a just and humane society.

The death penalty brutalizes life. It fails to recognize society's corporate responsibility for the distortions that appear in any one of society's children. The death penalty historically falls heaviest on the poor and the illiterate, both of whom have limited resources and limited access to legal representation. Sometimes the penalty has been exacted upon those who were later discovered to be innocent. Finally it violates the sacredness of life, for if life is holy, if our right to it is inalienable, then the most miserable specimen of human life shares this holiness even if he does not honor it.

I was once a prison chaplain to an inmate on death row who was later executed. Nothing about that experience was anything but brutal, life denying, vengeful, and dehumanizing. It was life at its very worst. It repels me even today to recall it. "You shall not kill" for me must apply here also.

Let no one misunderstand this. I retain my passion for a just and safe society. Surely we must be concerned for the victims of crime as well as for the criminals. We cannot have a just society made up only of what conservatives call "fuzzy-minded liberals with bleeding hearts," who express compassion only for the criminal and forget the victim. Somehow that description appears frequently in political oratory and seems to elicit an affirmative response. Our lower nature, our base motives for revenge, can be and are expressed by the simplistic candidates who constantly campaign on a platform using the code words "law and order." We applaud no matter how incongruous.

I attended the annual Brotherhood Awards dinner of the National Conference of Christians and Jews some years ago only to discover that the governor of Virginia used this forum for an exercise in cheap political oratory. He called on us to get the criminal element and give them what they deserved, and the dinner guests applauded just before presenting awards to those who had contributed most to the ideal of brotherhood in that community that year. No one else seemed to think that this was incongruous. I sat in silence and ached for the Commonwealth of Virginia.

The Hebrews, I am convinced, would have felt the incongruity of that moment, for the Commandment not to kill is not just a law to curb our own jealousy and hatred, though that is important; it is also a call to a new humanity. It is the code of the Covenant people. It is for those who have been touched with grace, called to a new being, chosen, elected, redeemed. Those who were no people—slaves in Egypt—but who now have been made into a special people, embraced by love, they are to live out a new humanity that is not ruled by envy, jealousy, or hostility.

"You shall not kill" finally fades into a positive command. You shall give life even at the cost of your own—for this is the highest form of humanity. This is the ultimate expression of the new creation. This is God's call that accompanies the demands of the Covenant.

On this level we can look anew at the Christian Lord Jesus. He was so alive to the reality of God, so transparent to the love of God, so at one with the life of God that we Christians assert that God was his very meaning. All the human bitterness, the rivalry, jealousy, envy, and human hostility is transformed in him into a life-giving power that accepts abuse, endures pain, allows death, and gives only love in return. This is what Jesus lived out. He was the new humanity, the new being, the full response to the Covenant, and as such the human face of the invisible God. In his life the final and deepest meaning of the sixth Commandment is seen, for you cannot give life by killing. But look at the victim dead upon the cross who, nonetheless, is strangely alive and life giving, and then observe the victors who gaze upon his lifeless body and do not seem to recognize that they are the ones who are dead. Here we discover the depths of biblical truth, namely that it is not enough to obey the letter of the law but to feel the spirit of the law's intention. For that spirit finally calls us to live life and then to share life, without stopping to count the cost.

There are many other areas of life we could look at: abortion, euthanasia, war, segregation, saturation bombing, atomic weapons. Each needs to be examined in the light of the biblical insight into the sacredness of life. Each is tempered by a thousand circumstances. Each finally for Christians must be examined in the light of the cross.

"You shall not kill." It is not as simple as it sounds.

10

Bodies and Relationships

The last six Commandments in the twentieth chapter of the book of Exodus all govern interpersonal relationships. They cover the full range of human action and human emotions, and they reveal the Hebrew theological attitude toward life.

Commandment number seven, "You shall not commit adultery," plunges us inevitably into a consideration of sexuality, sexual ethics, and sexual practices. It rises out of the Judeo-Christian view of the sacredness of human bodies, the sacredness of human relationships, and the sacredness of personhood.

Adultery and sexuality are emotionally-charged subjects. Sex is power, and we all know that power. We all live with it. Some of us are afraid of that power, some of us are victims of it. In many ways sex stands at the center of our personhood and, try as we may, we cannot shunt it aside. I am not just human. I am a human male. There is an incompleteness about being either a human male or a human female that drives one sex toward the other. There is a yearning for union that is emotional and spiritual as well as biological. Sex is of creation, the Bible asserts, and therefore, sex is good, even though it can obviously be misused. Sex is a force in the human yearning for union. No one can live without coming to terms with his or her sexuality. We deal with it in many ways. We bridle sex, we channel it, we express it. We redirect it, discipline it, repress it, and enjoy it. But we cannot deny it.

Sex is a part of life. Sex participates in creation. Sex is a gift of God. Sexuality is obviously a central factor in the life experience of everyone. I do not believe that there is any sexual problem that I have not dealt with pastorally in some form in my more than twenty years in the ministry. I have faced heterosexual problems and homosexual problems of both males and females. I have confronted problems in men of impotence on the one hand and Don Juanism on the other; problems in women of unresponsiveness on the one hand and insatiable desire on the other; premarital pregnancies and postmarital childlessness. There were fetishes, perversions, rape, incest, infidelity, romantic attachments, affairs across racial lines, family lines, and generation lines. These and many others are human problems that emerge every day; and when one is a pastor, life, unperfumed, comes from lots of different directions.

Being a pastor means that one must seek to love, accept and forgive people where they are, not where the ideals of life say they should be. To apply moral precepts and rigid rules to hurting lives trapped in a compromised society is not to be righteous, but rather to be hostile. I am not a situationist in the sense that I do take seriously the eternal principles as expressing the wisdom of the ages in the normal circumstances of life. Yet as a pastor I have learned that there are a myriad of exceptions to the ultimate rules which in the midst of life's complicated contingencies force people to choose, not from ideal options, but from available options.

We live today with new realities that have fueled a sexual revolution. These realities affect our standards, our values, our choices. The task of the Christian today is not well served by remaining ignorant of these realities or by seeking to ignore them. Perhaps what I am suggesting is that there is a very large area between what we would call ideal and what we would call immoral. In that gray area debate rages, choices are complicated, and human beings wrestle with a conflict between a search for wholeness and a reality of guilt.

Before seeking to examine the framework that provides the modern context for our decisions in the area of sexuality, let me make it quite clear where I stand.

Sex has its only fully proper place for me inside marriage where commitment is both deep and eternal. Sexual relationships between a husband and a wife can participate in the meaning of communion that reaches the edges of holiness and has something of the nature of a sacrament about it. Here life is shared in a way that it is shared nowhere else. This is the ideal, the goal, the hoped for pattern in marriage and in life. But this ideal is rare if it exists at all. Even though I have seen some wondrously happy married couples, most of the marriages I have worked with were struggling to find even vestiges of joy. Sexual problems were and are frequently both the focal point of tension and the bearer of destructive feelings. I am not one who would say that I approve of sexual relations outside of marriage, but I have come to be less judgmental and more compassionate; I have come to understand behavior patterns as appropriate for some people in some circumstances even though they could never be called ideal nor could they ever be fully acceptable to me or for me. Nothing said later in this chapter should be read except in terms of this guiding principle.

Yet it is obvious to me that we must find a place between the sexual ethics of yesterday, which were based upon a cultural and religious repression, and the sexual ethics of many people today, which suggests that "if you enjoy it it must be good." Yesterday's repression has lost its power, today's hedonism has lost all standards. Surely there is another alternative.

Let me begin by trying to dispel some of the fear. The dynamic motivating power of sex has, beyond the moral questions, biological and psychological dimensions which must be studied and understood. To ignore these dimensions is not to be moral; it is to be naive. To take cognizance of new insights into human sexuality from the life sciences is not, as some critics suggest, to contribute to the breakdown of morality. It is rather to find a new way to sail through uncharted seas developing a moral code that is in touch with both our deeper Christian convictions and the reality of this generation. Repression will not keep the genie of sex in the bottle in the twentieth century. Indeed those people who are so afraid of exploring a new basis for sexual morality might well examine their own unconscious motivation, for fear frequently masks desire which is regarded as unacceptable; when the superstructure of repression is threatened that fear becomes violent anger. We see this frequently because one of the facts that we have to face is that, whether we like it or not, yesterday's repressive patterns do not govern or control sexual behavior today.

To plunge into this subject is like facing delicate surgery. We must divide Christian principles from the cultural accretions of the ages that have become attached to them.

First we go to the historic context of this commandment itself. The seventh Commandment, "You shall not commit adultery," comes to us from a people who for many years after this Commandment was given still practiced polygamy, not monogamy. Monogamous marriage is not the original context of this injunction against adultery. This Commandment was given, according to the tradition of the Hebrew people, in the wilderness somewhere around the year 1250 B.C. Solomon, with his three hundred wives and seven hundred concubines, reigned from 961 to 922 B.C. That is the first fact we need to embrace.

Second, this law was received in, and influenced by, a patriarchal society, and the biblical record of that society at that time is quite clear that, even with this Commandment on their law books, the Jews did not regard sexual intercourse between a married man and an unmarried woman as an offense. For documentation see Genesis thirty-eight, which tells of Judah's affair with Hirah, an Abdulamite who is described only as his friend, even after he has had three children by her. Or see Judges Twenty-one, where the men of Benjamin seduce first and marry second. In the Hebrew idiom, reflecting the patriarchal system, a man committed adultery only if he took another man's wife; that is, for a man adultery was an offense against another's marriage rather than against one's own. A married woman, on the other hand, committed adultery if she was unfaithful with any man whether he was married or not. Thus, if a married man avoided married women, he could have as many affairs as he wished and still not violate Commandment number seven. Indeed, you can find in the biblical law that the seduction of a man's unbetrothed daughter was regarded simply as a minor offense against his property, not a violation of the seventh Commandment. That is the literal biblical context.

Now, within that narrow scope, adultery—that is, sex by a married man with someone else's wife or sex by a married woman with anyone other than her husband—was condemned and the guilty person was sentenced to death. The Hebrew word for adultery used in this Commandment was *na'aph*, and this word could apply to either a man or a woman.

The third thing that we must note is that the negative, repressive attitude toward sex that marks moralistic legalism is clearly not biblical. There is no such thing as a puritanical Hebrew. There is no Jewish Queen Victoria. There is no disparagement of the body or exultation of the soul in Hebrew thought. That comes from another tradition, and it is alien to the Bible.*

The Hebrews were a lusty life-affirming people, and their literature reveals and revels in this attitude. When I lived in Richmond, Virginia, I taught a Bible class that was broadcast over a local radio station each Sunday. On one occasion the radio station managers bleeped my broadcast because in their judgment the words being used were offensive to their listeners' ears. Much to their surprise and chagrin, they discovered that what they had censored was a passage I read verbatim from the Bible. (The King James Version at that!) The Song of Solomon—which is what I had been reading—is not discreet in extolling the physical beauty of a woman's body.

> Thy lips are like a thread of scarlet. Thy temples are like a piece of pomegranate. Thy neck is like the tower of David. Thy young breasts are like two roes that feed among the lilies. How fair is thy love, my spouse. How much better is thy love than wine and the smell of thine ointments than all spices. Thy lips drop as the honeycomb. Honey and milk are under thy tongue. Open to me, my love, for my head is filled with dew and my locks with the drops of the night.

These excerpts from chapters four and five of the Song of Solomon capture much of the Hebrew attitude toward bodies, toward sexuality, toward the beauty of the feminine form. Please note also that these words are seldom read in church,

---

*For a more detailed treatment of this subject see Chapter 3 of my previous book, *This Hebrew Lord* (New York: The Seabury Press, 1974).

even less seldom preached on by the clergy unless allegorized in a wild and irrelevant exegetical exercise.

The anti-body, anti-sex attitude that equates sexual intercourse with defilement, that exalts virginity as the highest vocation, is not now and never has been Hebraic.

To separate conventional religious attitudes from the Judeo-Christian revelation is to begin to understand that the repressive moralism against which our culture is in such rebellion is not necessarily Christian or biblical at all. Repressive moralism is a product of the dualistic Greek mind, which tended to denigrate the physical and material as less worthy than the nonphysical or spiritual. This dualism reached its zenith in Western civilization when it combined with a puritan zeal that was thorough in removing beauty and fun from life in every aspect, in instituting and institutionalizing the repressive mentality, and in identifying Christianity with a strict moralism and a rigid austerity. Remember that it was Queen Victoria, who, though having had nine children (which proved she made love to Prince Albert once in a while), was nonetheless "not amused" by any references to sex. Sexual repression was the unquestioned rule of the day, at least in "proper" society. It was, in fact, a mark of good breeding, at least for the women of that generation.

This attitude toward physical life that made a virtue out of repression was thus embraced by a moralistic Christianity to become the powerful, controlling superstructure that held the sexual drives of human beings in check. Perhaps this was necessary in that day to preserve the orderliness of society, the sacredness of the family, the morality of the culture. But such an attitude surrounded sex with fear and negativity. It assumed that sex was evil or animal in nature. It created guilt about feelings that are as natural as night following day, and it set the stage for a rebellion led by Sigmund Freud, the end of which we have not yet experienced. Indeed, the more powerful and repressive the superstructure, the more overwhelming has been the rebellion. Perhaps in the Victorian age sex could not have been managed in any other way. They could tolerate nothing short of the ideal and organized life to uphold that ideal and to minimize any deviations.

All kinds of social and religious pressures were created to keep this delicate balance. Childbirth out of wedlock was the infinite disgrace to the family. It marked the unwed mother for life. Such a sexual profligate was assured of hell, said the Church. Social diseases were also violent and fearful and were thought to be nothing less than punishment from God for violating the moral code. A limerick popular at that time went like this:

> *There was a young lady named Wilde*
> *Who kept herself quite undefiled*
> *By thinking of Jesus*
> *and social diseases*
> *And the fear of having a child.*

The triple terrors of sexuality fed the repression, and those triple terrors were quite simply "detection, conception, and infection." A tremendously powerful chaperon system was developed to insure virginity. This era recognized the power of the sexul drive and made the effort to place sexual acts into a context where they could be preserved in sanctity until they could be expressed in marriage.

Public opinion and religious attitudes combined to make sex, save in the context of marriage alone, the worst of all possible sins and the major area of moral concern. In puritan times adultery was punishable by death while child-beating was only considered unfortunate. Sex was placed under rigid control, and no one stopped to examine whether or not such a position was true to our biblical heritage; it was simply assumed that this was "Christian."

It is interesting to note that Jesus had nothing to say in any of the four Gospels about such things as sexual manners in courtship. Wherever we have very clear rules about that, we have something to which the culture has given birth; it cannot be rooted in the Christian Gospel itself.

Similarly, Jesus had nothing to say about perversion. He had nothing to say about masturbation, reproduction, birth control, or abortion. All we have on any of these subjects is tradition. This is not to say that the tradition is wrong, but that there is no word from the Lord that authoritatively places each of these vital issues of our age into a right and wrong situation even for Christians.

Though we have no record that Jesus was ever married, he certainly does not make a virtue of celibacy. He frequented parties, including weddings. The analogy of a marriage adorns many of his parables. He refers to himself in some instances of his teachings as "the bridegroom." I can find nothing anti-physical or anti-sexual in the New Testament. There is a healthy respect for the reality of sex. There is the necessity of guarding sex from abuse, but there is no negativity toward sex. That attitude is a modern Western creation. I must conclude that the cultural attitude toward sex, in terms of legalistic moralism, is not the Judeo-Christian attitude toward sex at all, but is rather a reflection of the way that an earlier era of our history related to the circumstances of sex. I do not mean to criticize or condemn that era. I only mean to say that, given their reality, given their circumstances, that was the way they chose to deal with that problem.

If the reality changes, however, then the way we deal with that reality must change. That is what has happened in the area of sex in the last one hundred years. The circumstances have changed; the reality has changed. The attitudes of the past are not wrong but they were created to deal with circum-stances that no longer exist. Thus, we are left with the situa-tion of having a new reality without having any new way of relating to it.

There are four major new factors that affect sexual behavior in the twentieth century. First, whether we like it or not, sex and procreation are no longer necessarily linked. Love-making and baby-making can, in fact, be separated, and that means inevitably that the whole superstructure set up in order to keep babies from being born out of marriage no longer pos-sesses the same urgency, and consequently, no longer can un-dergird sexual practices with the same power.

A second fact has changed: one hundred years ago, puberty occurred in boys and girls much later than it does now. The average age was sixteen or seventeen, and marriage, particu-larly of girls (at least in the dominant strata of society which set the norms), generally took place one or two years after puberty. The time of virginity thus was quite brief. Today, puberty takes place at age eleven or twelve, and marriage, somewhere between twenty-one and thirty. How "natural" is sexual abstinence from puberty to marriage in such a long culturally imposed separation? What is the emotional and physical price that virginity requires in this kind of world and are we prepared to pay it? These issues must be weighed by those who would set moral standards.

The third new reality: in the highly mobile culture of the automobile, the chaperon system of a hundred years ago is impossible. With external controls greatly diminished, we begin to depend on building internal controls to protect one's "honor" and "virtue." If internal repressive controls are too rigid, the price in physical and emotional health may be costly. One may not be able to turn these rigid controls off as soon as marriage occurs; if they continue to operate, they will create a host of problems. No one would regard that as a desirable state.

The fourth new reality is that the powerful fear of infection which inhibited or at least deterred sexual activity in previous years can, since the advent of the miracle drugs, be successfully controlled. In previous eras the social diseases were devastating in their effect, producing sterility, abscesses, brain damage, mental illness, and sometimes even death. The religious attitude of repression treated these physical diseases quite simply as the visitation of the wrath of God upon those who were immoral. Mentally disturbed people who were victims of syphilis were, in earlier times, the primary inhabitants of our mental institutions. This is no longer so.

We live today with the new realities of the twentieth century, a century that has separated procreation from sexual activity, stretched the time between puberty and marriage to ten years or more, removed the chaperon system, and to a large degree taken away the fear of infection. In the process we have rendered the repressive superstructure of yesterday irrelevant at best, even though its goal may still be highly desirable. It is crumbling before our eyes and, like Humpty Dumpty, all the king's horses and all the king's men will never put it together again. Now we must deal with sexual activity on a new basis that takes cognizance of our new reality.

So questions arise. What is the basis for sexual morality for

Christians in this age? Is there an area between the ideal and the immoral where sexual relations between consenting unmarried adults who are deeply committed to each other could be viewed in some way other than as destructive or wrong? Can we look at such relationships without moralistic judgment? Can we understand even if we do not ultimately approve? Can sexual activity apart from the holiest context of marriage ever be more positive than negative? Can it in some conceivable set of circumstances enhance life more than it destroys life? Is repression or abstinance the only choice a Christian ethic can tolerate for widows, widowers, unmarried adults or divorced people?

On what basis can one walk through these questions as a Christian? There must be guidelines that we can find to direct us to some ethical stance that, though short of the ideal, is still not just a reflection of yesterday's repressive system, for that simply will not win today's world. The guidelines for a Christian must, I am convinced, exclude promiscuity. There must be a position that is true to the twentieth-century reality and yet still takes seriously the sacredness of marriage, and this is what contemporary Christians must seek. What does the Commandment "You shall not commit adultery" mean today, within the reality of the twentieth century, the situation in which you and I are now living? Even more importantly, what does it mean in terms of the situation that our children are now facing? How can we maintain character and commitment and oppose mutual using in the name of love? For such are part of a Christian's concept of life.

I cannot speak definitively, but I can share with you the guidelines that I have discovered which have helped me personally and as a pastor to chart a path through this world. These are guidelines that I think can be grounded in the Christian revelation.

First, sex is not evil; it is good. It should therefore not be *re*pressed; it is meant to be *ex*pressed. But the expression of this good gift must come inside a relationship through which it can communicate the holiness of life as well as the gratification of biological desire.

Second, the holiness of life and the gratification of biological desire cannot be separated without dehumanizing people.

Third, no pattern of sexual behavior that is counter to natural biological forces will ever succeed, except by inflicting vast distortions upon the personhood of the one who is a victim of such a repressive moralism.

Fourth, marriage is, I believe, the context in which sex finds its holiest and most life-giving outlet.

Fifth, marriage is sacred. Fidelity to the marriage vows is an essential ingredient in the development of character, in the function of parenthood, and in the stability of society. To violate this fidelity in marriage is to run incredible and enormous risks of destruction of essential human meaning. Therefore, only for the most compelling and unusual circumstances could such sexual infidelity by a married partner ever be justified. These reasons must be far deeper than boredom and far deeper than the oft-repeated "My wife doesn't understand me," or "My husband no longer pays any attention to me." There is no normal biological need in any human being that cannot be met inside the sexual exclusiveness of marriage. There is no biological necessity for a variety of sexual partners. Nothing but the human ego is involved in the incessant desire for new thrills and new conquests, which are designed basically to overcome one's own psychological doubts and fears of sexual dysfunction.

Sixth, the ultimate Christian ethic is not rooted in sexual abstinence. It is rooted in the fullness and holiness of life. Sexual indiscretions are not the most profound transgression even though they are transgressions. At its best, sexual fidelity is an asset to the fullness of life, but there are rare occasions when the two are in conflict, and when that time comes, the call to the fullness of life, I believe, takes priority in the Christian scale of values. Let me illustrate this with a premarital and a postmarital situation.

I am the father of three daughters. I love and admire those three girls inordinately. I want for them all the sweetness that life offers. As I have previously stated, I am a rather old-fashioned man and an old-fashioned father. On my scale of values, premarital virginity has an important place. It is not *the* primary value, but it is a high value. My primary goal is to raise my daughters to be whole persons, complete women, loving themselves, rejoicing in their femininity, proud of their bodies, capable of entering the bond of marriage and the bed of marriage with confidence, anticipation, joy, and abandon; free to give and to receive, free to be fulfilled and to fulfill, free to explore the mystery of sex with their husbands, exalting in the love that gives life and produces life. That is my primary goal. If they can have all of this and still be virgins at the time of their marriage, I would consider that the best of all possible worlds. If they cannot, for me, the fullness of life would take the highest priority.

If the price of virginity is the repression and distortion of that which is good and wondrous; if virginity is achieved by surrounding sex with guilt and fear; if the quest for virginity drives them to an unhealthy dependency on some form of autoeroticism as a preferred means to release their sexual energy; then for those reasons I would say the price of virginity is too high on my scale of values.

I want to make it clear that I do not in any sense regard masturbation as evil or destructive. I consider it a natural part of the discovery of bodily joys. Harm comes from masturbation only because of the fear and negativity with which past generations regarded it. I am impressed by some recent studies that seem to indicate that better marital adjustments are made by those who had regularly engaged in adolescent masturbation than by those who had not. Danger arises when one limits his or her sexual desire to this level, substituting a solitary act for the sharing of life which I believe is inherent in sexuality and is potentially the deepest human experience of community.

I have a great desire to keep an open and honest relationship with my daughters that would enable us to discuss all aspects of sexuality as I think parents should. If that discussion leads to the conclusions that sex before marriage is inevitable and, in their minds, desirable in their individual particular circumstances, then I would want each of my daughters to be well advised professionally and to have access to the best contraceptive devices available. I do not believe that the risk of conception is ever proper or ever loving outside the bond of marriage.

If the ideal cannot be lived out then I would hope that neither my daughters nor any other young man or woman would engage in premarital sexual relations except as the result of the most mature act of decision-making. I think that such relations must wait until he or she is capable of handling the full emotional demands of that activity and must occur only inside a very special relationship where love, trust, commitment, and deep communication already exist. For me this is still marriage, but it is not for many living in today's world. Without these conditions, sex seems to me to be a mutual using of two persons, an activity destructive of character, and a violation of the holiness of life. Whenever sex is these things, it cannot help but be wrong, for it destroys rather than creates life. My ultimate standard of moral judgment is found when I face the questions: Does this act bring life or does it bring death to the persons involved? Does it enhance being or does it repress being? Does it make the people involved more capable of giving love or does it make them less capable of giving love? My ultimate ethical standard is the development of the fullness of life for every person. It is not found in any rule that begins with the words "You shall not," for life as I know it as a pastor, with real human beings facing real human circumstances in specific situations, is far too complex for that; yet the "you shall nots" still define the normative ethical pattern reflecting the wisdom of the ages.

Moving on to problems of a later stage of adult life, let us first examine the role of the single adult—unmarried, widowed, or divorced. If a single adult simply cannot live the celibate life and is not willing to be married or is simply not emotionally ready for or capable of marriage what are the alternatives that could still be called moral? Do we want to be in the position of saying that the satisfaction of sexual desire alone is an adequate basis for marriage? Do we have any alternative other than the denial of sexual energy or the repression of sexual desire? Must we as Christians offer only an ideal or a word of judgment? Is not our gospel more loving than that? In previous eras sexual prohibition was decreed for "maiden ladies," at least for proper maiden ladies, and they endured it frequently by becoming the paradigms of rigid virtue with ramrod backbones and judgmental airs, in many instances, enough to create a recognizable caricature. They were both vicious gossips and fierce, self-appointed guardians of the community's righteousness. No other possibilities were open to them so they convinced themselves of the rightness of their stance and society enforced their role by applauding it publicly. One wonders about the inner sadness that many of these women have endured. Today we question whether that is the only option and at the very least today's society will not affirm the "maiden lady syndrome" of yesteryear. A post-Freudian society is not likely to make a virtue of rigid repression. No such burden was laid on the single male, and it was the normative practice for him to find sexual outlet among the lower-class women of the society. In previous generations, the divorced person was almost nonexistent, so scandalous was divorce in that era, and the widowed person was thus the only remaining single adult.

Today few people in psychological or medical circles would suggest that widowhood at age thirty-five, for example, means that the spouse must cap his or her sexual energy forever. Sexual needs do not die with the death of one's husband or wife. Yet when there was no way to separate sex from procreation, this may have been the only alternative. The price a man or woman paid may well have been an increasingly bitter personality, a frustration that even led to physical disorders. That may have been the best alternative years ago, but is that the best or the only alternative today? If the fullness of life is the goal of the Christian gospel, sexual abstinence may not always serve the goal; we may have some other options. Must sexual relations between consenting, unmarried adults always be considered wrong? Are there at least some instances that could be seen as beautiful and life-giving, beneficial and fulfilling, an enhancing of one's being, even if not ideal? If so what would be the necessary conditions for this result?

As a Christian pastor who has faced this problem with people many times, I would say that the following guidelines are absolutely essential. Sex between unmarried adults might be inside that gray area between the ideal and the immoral if, first, no one's marriage is being violated by either party; second, if it is a union of love and caring, not just a union of convenience and desire; third, if sex is shared only after other things have been shared, other things such as time, values, friendship, communication and a sense of deep trust and emotional responsibility; fourth, if it is both loving and discreet, private, shielded from those who would not or could not understand; if it is valued as a bond between the two people involved and between them alone, never violating the sacredness of the exclusive quality of that moment.

If the fullness of life is the goal, and if the sexual options are abstinence that cannot be managed without physical distress and impairment of personality, or an affair under the circumstances which I have just outlined, then I believe that an affair might be for some people the best option, the most life-giving. Therefore, under these circumstances, sexual intercourse outside of marriage could be good and not bad even though I would still not call it ideal.

Consider the final gray area. What about sex outside of marriage when the marriage itself is still in force? I cannot see how that could be good or desirable except under very extreme circumstances. If the marriage dies sexually, then before one partner or the other can justify an extramarital affair, I believe that he or she is bound to seek outside help and to work on that sick marriage. If the partners do not do this, they cannot possibly do anything but violate their word, their character, and their fidelity in a sexual union outside of marriage. There is no way, in my mind, that one will find support for that kind of behavior in the Christian Gospel or in what I would call the ethics of life, which grow out of that Gospel.

The fact that a wife has lost interest in sex or a husband has become impotent is a situation that cries out for professional help. It is not license for an affair. Yet there are rare circumstances where one partner or the other is rendered sexually incompetent by physical disease, accident, or by mental illness, so that the remaining partner is forced to choose between abstinence and the violation of the sacred bond of marriage. If the remaining partner can manage abstinence without destroying his or her life, I am convinced that that is the best course. But if he or she cannot, then what are the options in that gray area between the ideal and the immoral? There is the sheer physical release of autoeroticism, which is a lonely, shal-

low, non-life-giving possibility. Someone has called masturbation the ultimate sacrament of loneliness. It is a temporary
solution at best.

To avoid autoeroticism lonely people have sought sexual
outlet with prostitutes. But life is not found here either, for sex
is one human being sharing with another on the deepest level,
and this is patently impossible when love and community are
separated from sex or when one relates to a sex partner as a
thing, as impersonal as a partner from a rent-a-body agency.
I cannot see life developing in relationships with a prostitute,
indeed I think life is destroyed in such relationships. Therefore this falls out of the gray and into the immoral area.

The third option could be an occasional one-night stand,
wherever convenient, with a series of acquaintances. This is
only slightly different from prostitution. For sex to be sacrament of wholeness, it must be shared inside a relationship that
is special and loving. Shallow sexual contact with a variety of
partners cannot help but result in questions of identity and of
the meaning of love itself.

The last alternative could be an affair with one you love,
with whom you share many things, an affair discreetly carried
out with no threat of revelation, with no demands other than
the beauty of those special moments together. If the fullness
of life is the basis for Christian ethics, in some circumstances
—very special and extreme circumstances—I would suggest
that this latter alternative might be, for these very rare few,
the best of the available options. But let it be stated clearly that
no living or potentially living marriage could ever be violated
by either partner in these circumstances, with this reasoning.
We are talking about an unusual exception to the rule. But as
a pastor I have had to confront such extreme exceptions more
than once. I have been driven to seek loving alternatives short
of the ideal but hopefully also short of the immoral.

I began this chapter by stating that through my experience
as a pastor I have been moved out of a rigid, moralistic legalism
into what I believe is a more loving and more compassionate
attempt to discover the best alternative within the particular
circumstances of each person's life. I reject a rigid ethical
system that applies a rule indiscriminately as one would place

a cookie cutter down on dough cutting it wherever it happens to land, whether it fits or not. I also reject the neo-hedonism that suggests that pleasure is the ultimate arbiter of what is right and what is wrong.

Christianity need not be tied to the repressive legalism of yesterday that is not biblical and that is not essential in the reality of the twentieth century, yet Christianity does have standards and norms that must be heard in the midst of the moral revolution today. I have tried to spell out these standards as I understand them. Even if new forms for marriage contracts or family structure develop into the norm of the future, these standards will still be relevant for they center on the sacredness of life.

"You shall not commit adultery" invites us to look at the depth of human personhood, the depth of human relationships, the sacredness of human bodies, the biological fact that sex is powerful, and to decide how love and life and being can be expressed so as to glorify the Creator in every act of the creature. Christians in the twentieth century need to bear their unique witness in word and deed in this arena of human sexuality.

11

Stealing in Microcosm and Macrocosm

We come next to a Commandment that can be as simple or as profound as one wants to make it. "You shall not steal," Commandment number eight.

Originally it referred to both a human and a material object. To steal a human life, of course, was kidnapping, and that was not a rare practice in the ancient world, where children were often stolen and placed into indentured servitude. The Hebrew people, a people who had been born in slavery, were not likely to tolerate a practice which led to any new enslavement, but as kidnapping became a rarer and rarer phenomenon, this Commandment more and more came to be viewed exclusively in terms of the sacredness of property and possessions, and the right to privacy.

Basically and on its simplest level, it means "You shall not take what is not your own." On a deeper and more profound level, however, this Commandment raises searching questions about how we define, in mass society, what constitutes that which is our own, raising the whole area of tension and conflict between that which is in the private domain and that which is in the public domain. It forces us to examine the meaning of private property and the issues of our stewardship over the physical resources and the means of production in our world. It brings into focus the whole question of an equitable tax structure in a just society. All of these issues are the legitimate domain of one who would search out the depth of meaning behind the Commandment "You shall not steal."

Dr. Joseph Fletcher, in his book *Moral Responsibility*, distinguishes between what he calls "microethics"—that is, ethics seen in microcosm, particularly in terms of personal behavior patterns—and "macroethics"—that is, ethics that are seen in macrocosm, involving the whole society. Microethics are the personal acts of an individual, his or her personal gifts of charity and personal works of love. Macroethics are the corporate acts of the whole culture, which should be designed to build a just society. They redress the balance of grievances and create a wholesome and socially sensitive world for all who share in it, so that the situations that produce the need for individual charity and individual works of love might be eliminated or at least minimized. Both microethics and macroethics are important. I would like to explore both levels as we view the eighth Commandment, "You shall not steal."

First, let us examine this Commandment on the microethical level. What each of us possesses is, in a way, a part of our deepest self. Our sense of justice demands that there be a general respect for property, that there be a strongly accepted public sensitivity which proclaims a sanctity of ownership. Otherwise, there is chaos, anarchy, and distrust in the society, and the painful necessity to be perpetually on guard to protect what is our own.

When any society loses this tenet of corporate faith, this level of corporate trust, then the crime level soars, and people are reduced to employing burglar alarm systems, arming themselves to the teeth, taking pistol-firing instructions, and installing padlocks, living as if they expect to be robbed. When those symptoms appear in the life of a society, then that society is in a state of serious, maybe even fatal, sickness. No amount of increased police protection or political oratory about law and order will ever heal that sickness. Police protection and political oratory simply do not reach the level from which the problem arises. What these symptoms reveal is nothing less than the breakdown of the cultural values that glue society together, because in that society there is no longer a culturally accepted norm for what is right and what is wrong. There is no longer a generally accepted assumption that private property is sacred; and something radical needs to be done to reestablish the social fabric, the values of that society, or that society will not endure.

On a radical level the citizens of that society need to commit themselves corporately to see that, in the legal structure of that society, the legitimate needs of those who feel dispossessed are met. They must give hope where hopelessness has taken over and create opportunity where doors have been slammed shut.

No society can or will survive unless there is a wide acceptance of certain cultural values. If those elements of the population for whom crime is an acceptable alternative grow to any sizable percentage because of economic privation or because of prejudice, or if these alienated groups are prevented from finding a way to work within the system, then the whole society will be reduced very quickly to choosing between living in a police state or living in anarchy. That is a dreadful choice. However, in urban America today, that is increasingly the choice we have before us, and in that choice there is no doubt in my mind but that America will choose a police state, even the security of the Mafia, for historically security is always chosen over freedom. Freedom is considered a luxury in human life, perhaps the world's greatest luxury; but security is an absolute essential. Hopefully we can find that we can have security with freedom, which is, of course, the best possibility. Freedom is not and cannot be achieved unless the society is based on justice, radical justice, in which the worth of every life is equally affirmed. Only in such a society can those who would break the cultural norm and violate the society's rules be minimized so that minimum police protection will be required and no interference with the essential freedom of life will be necessary.

When a society agrees on its norms for collective living, inevitably it lays these rules down on stone, as it were, inside the society's code of law. Now in a democracy that code can always be changed by the elected representatives who, in fact, represent the will of the people so long as there is a constitution that forbids the exploitation of the minority. Therefore the law has a certain flexibility in a living society.

Inside the code of every people, however, whether that code be ancient or modern, Western or Eastern, capitalist or communist, there is incorporated a law against taking by force or stealth what is not one's own, what one has not earned, and what one has no natural right to claim, for that is what stealing is. Stealing comes in lots of sophisticated forms: burglary, larceny, embezzlement, hijacking, skyjacking, shoplifting, plagiarizing, gypping, looting, swindling, cheating, deceiving, concealing defects, false labeling, giving short measures, exaggerating quality. Stealing comes in the dishonest claims of false advertisement, in not doing an honest job, in not paying an honest wage.

When I lived in Tarboro, North Carolina during the late fifties, I could employ full-time domestic help for eighteen dollars a week. I was insensitive to what I did. For me, that was the going wage in the economic law of supply and demand, but in fact, that was part of the exploitation of the weak by the strong. It was robbery. It was stealing just as surely as it would have been if I had held up the local bank. I regard the minimum wage law as a protection against robbing a human life of its value, time, and dignity. I have noticed that it is never the poor who complain when the minimum wage is raised.

There are so many other forms of stealing that are still on the microethical level. There is the taking advantage of ignorance; manipulating people to purchase expensive things in time of bereavement; preying on the distressed; welshing on a bet; doing shoddy workmanship; raising prices for windfall profit in times of shortages; having your child lie to get a cheaper rate; falsifying your income tax form, or estimating your deductions very liberally; manipulating long distance telephone lines to send messages without having to pay. To these examples (or their ancient equivalents) and countless others, the eighth Commandment called Israel and later called the Christian community to live out a standard of radical personal honesty in obedience to the God who established our Covenant.

"You shall not steal." Nothing in the balance of this chapter should in any way minimize the importance of this microethical level of behavior to which this Commandment spoke in the past and, I believe, still speaks today. We must however go deeper into what is specifically a biblical attitude toward property, both public property and private property, in order to examine the Commandment "You shall not steal" in a macroethical setting.

There is a legitimate asceticism within Christianity, but it is not an anti-materialism. Even after Christianity embraced the dualism of the Greek world, the mainstream of Christian ascetical life was still not completely anti-materialist. The monasteries, for example, emphasized personal poverty, chastity, and obedience, but they did not denounce communal wealth, and some of the monastic religious orders wound up in the pre-Reformation days with incredible wealth in land holdings, much of it confiscated in the battles between the various crowns and the papacy.

If one really believes in the Judeo-Christian doctrine of creation, which proclaims the holiness and the goodness of all life, including material life, then the ethical question of condemning material things does not arise. The ethical question arises rather out of proper or improper use of material things.

The Gospel does not distinguish between the haves and the have-nots nearly so much as between the have-too-muches and the have-not-enoughs. The Gospel recognizes that any material possession can be dangerous if we idolize it. Sometimes wealth does corrupt, and when it does it breeds greed, lust, and human insensitivity. Sometimes wealth also creates saints and benefactors and philanthropists. Sometimes poverty produces piety and a wondrous peace and freedom from the mundane. But other times poverty produces a bitterness and oppression, and the victim of poverty, unable to find a constructive outlet for his hostilities, seizes for himself the right to judge, and violates all the community standards of decency. The real ethical issue is how we use property both in scarcity and in abundance.

This realization drives us to the deeper ethical insight that the use of our wealth is one primary way we act out Jesus' summary of the Law, which certainly embraced the eighth Commandment, "You shall love your neighbor as yourself." It raises to a new level of consciousness the meaning of stewardship, making us ask very searching and uncomfortable questions like "Whose wealth is it, really?" and "Who is to be ministered to by this wealth?" An improper stewardship may constitute a violation of the Commandment "You shall not steal." I think that is an unavoidable conclusion.

It is the Judeo-Christian belief that, in the words of Holy Scripture, "The earth is the Lord's and all the fullness thereof." We human beings are, according to the Bible, acting on God's behalf as temporary stewards of what is primarily his and not ours. The things of God's world are ours to use, but as each decade goes by in our increasingly crowded world, it becomes more and more obvious that we are not free to do what we will with these things.

In mass society private property rights mean something very different from what they meant on the American frontier. Even the most conservative people will admit this when they rush to protect their neighborhoods with building codes that compromise the integrity of private property. A frontiersman of the Old West did not have to be sensitive to his neighbor ten miles away as we must be in housing complexes or on highway cloverleafs. In mass society we cannot escape interdependence. "The public interest" is a recognition of our common environment. We must also think of generations yet unborn before we pollute our rivers, lakes, and seas, and rob the land of its minerals and its capacity to sustain life. Acquiring wealth can no longer be the solitary goal of any business, large or small. Business must be socially sensitive to the price the society will have to pay today and tomorrow for those profits that overfeed, overindulge, and overpamper our generation.

Economics thus raise very serious moral issues which the Christian faith must address. Beyond that, other questions have to be faced. Questions such as: Do the natural resources of the earth belong to the God who created them to be used by all his children for their mutual benefit? Or do they belong to those who happen to own the land under which these resources are located? Do they belong to those who have the capacity to tap the resources—like offshore oil deposits, for example? Can the Arabs legitimately bring the whole world to its knees simply because the world's oil reserves are basically underneath Arab land? If one says, as Americans tend to, that anyone can own the resources of the earth simply because he or she owns the land over which those resources are located, then one must face more questions. What is the obligation of that assigned owner or that assigned developer to the society as a whole? Should limits be placed on the amount of wealth one person may accumulate from the resources of the earth? Should the stockholders of Exxon and Texaco be the primary beneficiaries of the offshore oil that lies, theoretically, under international seas? There also seems to be an incompatibility between the Christian faith and a society in which an individual like the late Howard Hughes could accumulate nearly two billion dollars during the same period of history in which the unemployment rate of the nation soared to nearly ten percent. There must be an appropriate balance between personal accumulation of wealth and public need.

Consider this in a total economic framework. Basically I believe in the free enterprise, capitalist system and its necessary corollary of private property. I believe in this system because I am convinced it is necessary to the psychological dimensions of human life, to the levels of personality from which human motivation finally springs. It is my theological sense of the doctrine of man which says that any system that expects to work with human nature must have some kind of incentives built into it, a profit motive for example, or adequate rewards for labor. A system that rewards industry and ingenuity provides that incentive. A complete state socialism does not seem to understand the nature of human life. Yet at the same time, an unbridled, completely laissez-faire capitalist system can be as destructive to human life and to human value as any communist system might be, for unbridled capitalism will inevitably grind to that point where the capitalists are very few, owning all the means of production, and the masses are many, and they are being exploited. This is exactly the stage that Karl Marx predicted would be ripe for revolution. Karl Marx never understood the ability of the capitalist system to correct its own abuses and to guarantee the good life for the masses of people.

I would say yes to capitalism but no to unbridled capitalism. The best friends that capitalism has in this country today are the antitrust laws, the graduated income tax, the inheritance taxes, the social security program, and all the other legislation that has tempered the capitalist system, spread the wealth, provided for adequate public services, and created the great middle class that makes the American economy strong.

There is an assumption in the American Constitution that rises out of a biblical insight into the nature of human life: given the self-centered, sinful nature of all human beings that causes us to operate from the vantage point of self-interest, no one person or one branch of government should ever be allowed to achieve total power. It is because we are self-centered that power corrupts and total power corrupts totally. Effective government, says our Constitution, must have a system of checks and balances, divided and, to some degree, autonomous branches with executive, legislative, and judicial functions. That is one truth the framers of our Constitution understood, and they understood it quite well.

Not quite so well did they understand two corollaries of that truth. The first is that whenever any life exists without any power, because of the sinful nature of all human life, that powerless life will be exploited. History documents this. History is the story of the exploitation of the powerless. When labor had no power, labor was exploited and we had sweat shops, starvation wages, long hours, and abusive child labor practices. In fact, John Locke, thought to be so enlightened a political philosopher and a champion of laissez-faire capitalism, wrote: "The children of the poor must be required to work in the industrial enterprise beginning at age three."

The second corollary is that when people—any people—are exploited, the seeds of revolution are at that moment being sown. Exploitation will not be tolerated by any human being forever, for it violates the sacredness, the image of God that is within us. Hence labor unions, which can confront owners with effective power, are an essential ingredient in a healthy capitalist society, for power must be shared in order to prevent exploitation. Exploitation is nothing less than a form of stealing. It is the stealing of a man's labor for the benefit of the owner. It is a social violation on the macroethical scale of the Commandment "You shall not steal."

I believe that enlightened Christians must seek to remove every vestige of exploitation from within their society. In obedience to this, Christians must oppose segregation at every level and in every form; they must support the rights of labor to organize for collective bargaining. Christians must support the intention of the Equal Rights Amendment and anything else which will stop the economic and sexist exploitation of women.

As a Christian, as a stockholder, and as one who believes in the American system, I also think it is a duty to raise serious questions about the ethical practices of some American companies which seem to be exploiting the natural resources of some of the small and powerless countries of the world, again sowing there the seeds of a deep enmity which we will someday have to reap. Those concerns I should voice legitimately through my right to speak and to vote at the annual meetings of the companies in which I own shares, for the primary purpose of business can no longer be only to make money. The purpose of business must include a sensitivity to the needs of the whole society, domestic and foreign.

Harry Emerson Fosdick, whom I quoted earlier, observed that the basic test of any society is what happens to the underdog. Good intentions will never protect the underdog. That is a kind of naive do-goodism. Only power will protect the underdog. A just society must organize itself so that no one is disenfranchised, no one is powerless; therefore exploitation will be kept at a minimum, and the society will remain healthy.

Beyond these things, a just society will require that an appropriate share of private wealth support the public needs of the whole society. A just society will levy appropriate taxes for this purpose, to support the best possible public systems, public parks, and playgrounds, schools, and health facilities. Taxes are needed to provide for the development of the arts—museums and symphony orchestras, for example—for the enrichment of the life of the public. The public need must always be balanced against private wealth. Where that exact balance is, every society must determine; but it is in the deepest vested interest of those who share most of this world's goods that they be the most concerned about the public welfare. It is interesting to me that, in the American political scene, the people of great wealth, like the Roosevelts and the Rockefellers, have tended to be liberal in their political thinking.

What does it say about the soul of a nation when, in an economic downturn, the leaders of that nation seek to balance the federal budget by cutting the school lunch program and the food stamp program, while at the same time maintaining a defense establishment that has five times as many admirals in the navy today as in World War II. What are these admirals admiraling, except a very top-heavy bureaucracy?

One of the great jobs of the institutional Church in our age should be to help this society reconceive and revalue its whole system of priorities. In our period of the economics of opulence, we may yet face a massive imbalance between material values and moral values, between private wealth and public need. We might even reach the point where our Christian consciences will force us to work for an increased tax upon our opulence, and that would really be to rise above our vested self-interest in order to provide the necessary public facilities and services for the whole society. To be very specific, I think the whole question of sales tax needs to be studied across the land. I would hope that commodities could be divided into three categories: necessities, desirable goods, and luxuries. I would remove the sales tax from necessities, leave it at the present level on desirable goods, and increase it substantially on luxuries. For example, I think there should be a higher tax on cars with unnecessarily large horsepower, because the whole society has to pay to clean up the polluted environment which they cause. I believe that there should be a substantially larger tax on high-test gasoline, clearly a luxury not a necessity.

My text for recommending these things would be nothing less than the eighth Commandment, raised to the macrocosmic level, "You shall not steal." Living in justice in this world as a good steward of God's bounty, maintaining privacy and yet caring for every legitimate public need, removing every vestige of exploitation, protecting the environment for today's and tomorrow's generations, and being honest in every individual transaction, all of these are covered when we push the Commandment "You shall not steal" into the very depths of our complicated and complex lives. Its echoes reverberate into every nook and cranny of our existence, and there is nowhere to hide. Those naive people who continue to parrot ridiculous statements like "the Church should stick to the Bible and not get involved with life" will be revealed for what they are, because what we believe and how we act on every level of life can never be separated. It is through politics and through economics as well as through personal morality that we are called to build a just society in which we love God with our hearts, our minds, our souls, and our strengths, and in which we love our neighbors as ourselves.

12

The Human Tongue—
A Call to Responsibility

The essence of the Jewish Law was codified in the memorable form that the Jews called the Ten Words. That was done many hundreds of years ago. These Ten Words were designed to govern the relationships between a person of the Covenant and the God of the Covenant and between two or more people within the Covenant. It is interesting to note that when the rules governing human behavior are reduced by the Hebrew people to the number of ten, no fewer than two of the ten have to do with human speech. "You shall not take the name of the Lord your God in vain." "You shall not bear false witness against your neighbor."

The capacity to speak, symbolized by the physical tongue, is the primary way through which we human beings express ourselves, and nothing reveals more deeply the biblical insight into the sinfulness and brokenness of human life than our verbal means of self-expression.

An ancient Talmudic story tells of a king who sent two of his servants out with very interesting instructions. One was asked to bring back the greatest thing that mankind has ever known, and the other was asked to bring back the worst and most destructive thing that mankind has ever known. Both, according to the story, returned with the human tongue.

From the tongue come forth the words that build relationships, express love, bring peace, pronounce blessings, call people into a fuller life—words that proclaim liberty. Parents separated from their children know the joy and meaning of a voice that seems to leap the vast expanse of distance via the telephone. It was the tongue that gave Socrates, Isaiah, Abraham Lincoln, and Winston Churchill their immense power and their tremendous gifts of leadership, for each of these people could move a nation simply with his speech. They could articulate the deepest yearnings of a people and galvanize the emotional resources of a nation.

However from the same human tongue also come lies and gossip, slander and curses, vilification and character assassination, cutting words and false witness, rumor and innuendo. The tongue expresses the inner being of a person better than anything else, so twice the Ten Commandments aim their insights at this member of the human body. When one takes the name of the Lord in vain, one reveals that he is separated from the deepest ground of his being; he is separated from God. When one bears false witness against his neighbor, he reveals that he is separated both from his neighbor and from himself. It is this insight that drives us into the biblical definition of sin, a definition that is far deeper than the behavior of human life, far deeper than the level of our deeds.

Biblical sin is a description of our human existence. Sin is the description of life that is lived separated from God, alienated from oneself, and cut off from one's neighbor. Sin is a description of life that is lived in inadequate love, an inadequacy that drives us constantly to seek affirmation. When one analyzes what might be called "the sins of the tongue," one sees this inadequacy and alienation in operation.

What is gossip, for example? It is more than the malicious word of one who seeks to do harm. Gossip is an insidious attempt by an insecure person to gain power. By passing on the gossip, a person is announcing not so subtly that he or she is important, "in the know," that he or she has secret sources of information. The more important the subject of gossip, the better the neurotic needs of the gossiper are served. Gossip columnists turn out their columns, whisper magazines turn out their scandal sheets, and insecure hearts of little people feed their sick souls on the results. They make these businesses into a million-dollar industry feasting on the private lives, mostly imagined, of public figures. There is a tremendous price to be paid for being a public figure. There is a price in dignity, privacy, and in the truth itself, because around every public figure are thousands whose insecurity feeds on the inner life of the public person.

There is one other level of gossip. When a person passes gossip, he is in fact cutting the victim down. In the heart of insecure human beings, cutting someone else down enables one to imagine that he or she can in fact build himself or herself up. By magnifying another's faults, I can minimize my own. Beneath the gossip that we hurl, sometimes in fun, sometimes in maliciousness, there is a broken, insecure, unloved life searching for importance, for being, for love. The tragedy of human behavior is that so long as we seek to build ourselves up, to overcome our deficiencies, we in fact only spin webs around ourselves, isolate ourselves more deeply than ever from one another, and reveal our desperate need for the love of God. One does not provide for himself or herself the love he or she needs by cutting someone else down. Thus both the victim of the gossip and the gossiper become victims of life. To the life victimized by the need to gossip, we hear the ninth Word of God, "You shall not bear false witness."

In addition to gossip, although frequently a part of it, is the human experience of falsehood we call "lying." What is a lie? Now obviously there are all kinds of gradations and motivations behind telling falsehoods. Let us get underneath the kind of mentality which says that you ought to be truthful to the point where it hurts, so you go to a party and say, "This is the lousiest party I've ever attended!" feeling virtuous because you are being honest.

What level of our being is served by our bending the truth? A lie is a way that we, in our insecurity, recreate the world of reality so that that world ministers better to our needs. We lie to enhance our image, to build our prestige, to overcome our sense of inadequacy. Hence all lying is finally self-serving, for if we enhance our image in our own eyes, we hope that we are doing the same in the eyes of others. We tell our falsehoods in such a way that we look better not worse. If we are going to lie about how big the fish we caught is, we never shrink the fish in the telling of the lie. But we do shrink our golf score. For an interesting insight into human nature, talk to some of those members of our society who, in fact, are constantly lied to, to the point where they have come to *expect* falsehood. Talk to a traffic policeman, for example, for these are among the world's most disillusioned people. Traffic policemen have been lied to so often by so many people in every strata of life that they trust no one. They expect to be lied to. So pervasive is this expectation that they are thrown for a loop if they ever happen to confront the truth.

Let me make a confession. A few years ago in the early winter I was stopped by a policeman in Richmond, Virginia on a Saturday afternoon. I was exceeding fifty miles an hour in a thirty-five mile zone. The red lights of his unmarked car began to flash, I pulled over, got out of the car, and went to confront my accuser, so that I was looking down on him instead of having him looking down on me. I had just come from a wedding, and was clad in the black clerical garb of my profession.

"What's your hurry, Reverend?" he asked.

"Do you want the truth or a wild story?" I inquired.

"The truth would be refreshing," he replied.

So I gave it to him. I said, "The truth is I just got through conducting a wedding, and I have been angry all day that anyone would be so insensitive as to schedule their wedding on the one Saturday in December when the Washington Redskins were playing the Dallas Cowboys in a return match, with a shot at the Super Bowl going to the winner." I told him that I knew that if I rushed home from that reception, I might get to see the last five minutes of that game. "That's why I'm speeding," I said.

There was a pause. "You know, Reverend," the policeman said smiling, "I think I understand that. That seems to ring true. I wouldn't want to hold you up any longer. Merry Christmas!"

Within the prescribed speed limits, I made it home. I saw the last five minutes, but the Skins lost, and it was a very black day.

To insecure people, who bend the truth to minister to the sense of human inadequacy, the ninth Word of the Lord says "You shall not bear false witness."

The Commandment against false witness originally had its setting in a court of law, before a bar of judgment. To lie when a man was on trial for his life, and the truth or falseness of the charges being investigated could cost him his life, was to strike a blow at the very heart of the system of human justice. It is no wonder that in many ancient societies one found guilty of false witness in a trial was punished severely. The Bible said that one who bore false witness would be punished with the same penalty as the person on trial would receive if convicted. The Romans would hurl the bearer of false witness to his death from a cliff. The Egyptians would cut off the nose and ears of one found guilty of bearing false witness in a trial. All of these were ways, some rather bloodthirsty, of recognizing that one who would destroy another person with a lie was a destructive element that society should not tolerate.

Lies, rumors, and innuendoes hurt. They hurt the victim, and they hurt the originator. They destroy the sacred fabric of life and the sacred fabric of trust, which are essential to our living together.

Again, a story from the Jewish tradition: Based on circumstantial evidence, a character-assassinating lie was told of a much-respected elderly man in a particular community. The victim, when he began to hear these things about himself, went and confronted his accuser with the facts that made the lie perfectly obvious. The originator of the juicy story apologized and asked if there was anything that he could do to right the terrible wrong that he had done. The elderly man, according to the story, walked into the bedroom and took a feather pillow from the bed. Taking out his knife, he split the pillow open, and then, going to the window of the second floor of his house, he dumped the feathers from that pillow into the breeze so they blew in every direction.

"Yes," he said. "There is something you can do. You can go out now and gather up all of those feathers and put them back inside this pillow."

"But, sir," the other man protested, "that is impossible. I could never recover each of those tiny feathers."

"Yes, it is impossible," the old man agreed. "Just as impossible as it is for you to take back all the hurt and the pain that your malicious rumor and absolute lie has done to me. You cannot recover the suspicion that you have sown, the damage to my character. That can never be undone."

Life is fragile. Truth is sacred. Character is always vulnerable to those who would wound it with false or malicious words; hence, the ninth Word of the Lord speaks to the destructive tongues residing inside the heads of insecure and sinful human beings: "You shall not bear false witness."

Thus far, we have examined this Commandment psychologically. Let me now drive this Commandment beyond that psychological point which gives insight into the nature of human life and try to arrive at another level. It is a complementary level concerned with the false witness that arises out of human ignorance. It is not the ignorance of not knowing enough facts, but the ignorance of being unaware of or insensitive to human nature. This is the kind of ignorance that feeds human prejudice, the kind of ignorance that distorts our objectivity and enslaves the human spirit. It is the kind of ignorance that perceives the partial and proclaims it to be the whole; that is unaware of its own subjectivity and therefore makes and repeats false and prejudicial assumptions; that cannot separate the truth of experience from the interpretation of that experience. On this level, all of us human beings are the victims of false witness as well as the bearers of false witness.

Let me illustrate what I mean. In a debate before the Executive Council of the national Episcopal Church a black man made some highly critical, judgmental statements about the United States of America. He, a citizen of this country, called this nation an "oppressive state," a state that broke the spirit of many of its citizens, grinding them under in a quest for profit. He was immediately challenged by an executive vice president of a major United States corporation, who extolled America's virtues as if God alone had created everything that was ours, and we were almost perfect. He lauded American business, making it appear to be the savior of the world. He minimized, if he even admitted, the faults of this land. He expressed the faith that even our minor faults were quickly being dealt with and would soon disappear.

As I listened to the debate, it was obvious that truth versus falsehood was not the issue here, even though both speakers were convinced of the objectivity of their thoughts. Rather, here were two competing conceptions of reality, both of which were true—true to the vision of the respective speakers but neither of which was necessarily true to the visions of the hearers.

The black man looked at the America of *his* experience, where a lid had been placed on his opportunities because he was black. It was an experience in which he had grown up in poverty, the poverty of second-class citizenship. He was allowed to vote only in the later years of his life. He was a product of a vastly inferior, segregated school system which used the hand-me-down textbooks that came from the white school system, while all the time listening to the white people proclaim that ours was a separate but equal school situation. This man's experience was that blacks are the last to be hired in properous times and the first to be laid off in depressed times. These were the eyes through which he looked at this nation. He watched American leaders go into a national panic when white unemployment reached six percent. But he knew that black unemployment never sank below ten percent; and among black males under twenty-five, unemployment has ranged up to fifty percent in some recent years.

This black man listened to white politicians talk about the abuses of the welfare system. He heard government leaders talk about balancing the budget by cutting back on the food stamp program, even while they rescued a struggling aircraft corporation with massive federal aid. This black man saw America open its heart to resettle thousands of Vietnamese refugees and to find jobs for them, even while the native black unemployment remained at an all-time high. The black citizenry watched these Vietnamese victims settle into homes in neighborhoods from which the black American population has been systematically excluded. Blacks watched minor concessions being made, token integration here and there, while the power base of the society changed very little. They saw segregation being preserved, even where it was no longer legal to do so. All the time these things were going on, the gap between the average white income and the average black income in this nation continued to widen, while the white population says such things as, "We have made significant progress in race relations in the last ten years."

This is the reality that this black man saw and out of which he spoke his critical and judgmental words about the America that he experienced. From where he stood, he thought his words were objective, for they were certainly real.

Then the executive vice president of the large corporation spoke out of his experience. He saw a very different United States. He saw a land of unlimited opportunity, where one with ability could climb the corporate ladder to success and affluence, for that was his experience. He saw the ingenuity and the ability of people being rewarded. His experience was of an America where genius meets opportunity and receives the good life as its prize.

He saw the great, affluent, prosperous middle class in this country being produced by a free economy, and he saw abundant resources being turned to alleviate the distresses of mankind.

Having never been the victim of prejudice, he tended to be judgmental about those who could not and did not make it within the system as he did. In all likelihood he might hold the view that those who do not succeed really were inferior. He was confident that people like himself who rule the business establishment do so because they have innate ability. He did not understand the distortion that enters the human spirit with prejudice. When this man heard America being criticized, nothing about that criticism rang true to his experience, and he responded by criticizing the first speaker. Instead of facing the issue, he sought to show him up as some kind of charlatan or revolutionary or communist.

Both of these viewpoints were accurate descriptions of the way each of these people had experienced the same nation. When they argued with each other, both of them were guilty of being ignorant. Both of them had taken their partial experience and elevated it to be the total experience. They were judging each other because they did not share the same vantage point. They were perfect examples of what it meant not to be aware of the realities of life, ignorant in the sense of being insensitive or of taking a partial experience and believing it to be the total experience of all human beings. These two men have identified their partial views and subjective experiences as objective truth. In the name of their angle of vision, without being aware of what they were doing, they were both bearing false witness against their neighbor.

The way I perceive reality is not the way reality is. The way you perceive reality is not the way reality is. That is a crucial distinction, a distinction that the ignorance of unawareness never quite comprehends. I see this in many shallow, affluent people who live their lives in the tiny circumscribed environment of the affluent suburbs. Their children go to the private schools; their social life revolves around the country club. They talk only to each other, and in their own narrow swath of life, they spend their time reinforcing one another's prejudices until they honestly believe that the majority of the world is white, Anglo-Saxon, affluent, and Protestant. Those who do not fit this mold, they seem to believe, exist to serve their convenience. They live as if it is their divine right to run the world.

To be unaware of the true dimensions of life, to be insensitive to the realities beyond your narrow little swath of existence, to talk to no one save the people who mirror your own prejudices back to you, to be the victim of your own narrow insecurity in life, this is to bear false witness just as surely as if you testified to the truth of a lie under oath.

When I lived in suburbia serving an affluent, socially uniform congregation, my primary experience socially was boredom. Every party we went to was attended by the same kinds of people, the same social strata. They looked alike, they acted alike, they talked alike. They drove the same cars, they liked the same kind of bourbon and scotch. They would say the same reinforcing things to each other week after week after week, and they never understood the meaning of life. They had limited themselves to a small piece of reality. It amazed me to watch a child of this environment spring loose and go off to a broad experience, and then come back home only to discover that their parents, grandparents, aunts, and uncles think the youth has been contaminated with "all that New York thinking." This, on a deeper level, is nothing less than the bearing of false witness.

To be very specific, I am convinced that this is also the particular and prevalent sin among those of us who call ourselves Christians. God can be experienced, but God cannot be explained. Words can point to God, but words can never capture God. Creeds can be formed to contain truths but creeds can never be formed that will exhaust the truth. God is bigger than the human frame of reference which tries to talk about him. God is bigger than any of the words of any human being about him. No matter how hallowed by the ages, no matter how thin or how gilt-edged the pages which we say contain the holy words, God is beyond the understanding of the Bible. God is beyond the understanding of our holy traditions, beyond the creeds, beyond the Church itself. No human system of thought can ever be ultimate. God, alone, is ultimate. Anything less than God will be destructive the minute we elevate it to the level of ultimacy. If you do not believe this, look at Christian history. Look at what we have done to human life in the name of the God of love. Christian history is dotted with the pock holes of the disastrous results of small minds who elevated their partial truths to the level of the ultimate, so that they could feel secure and be convinced that they were right. Then their religion became a club with which they beat into submission anyone who did not agree—and always in the name of God.

In my own tradition there seem to be those who are convinced that God is an Episcopalian. He isn't. Neither is God a Baptist or a Presbyterian or a Methodist or any of the other varieties of Christians that mark this nation's religious heritage. God does not prefer the King James Bible or the Book of Common Prayer. The Episcopal Church and the King James Bible and the Book of Common Prayer, I pray, all participate in and point to what God is, but God cannot be identified with those human things. The idolatry that grips the emotional lives of some people in religious matters is incredible.

Protestantism does not capture the truth of God. Neither does Catholicism. And while we're at it, let us be sure we understand that God is not an American; he is not white, black, or oriental. He is not a *he*. Yet each of these ways of describing him can, we hope, participate in the meaning of God. But please be aware of the limitations of human language and of human concepts.

God is not even a Christian. Christianity itself is also a human system, inspired of God, we pray, and so it is our attempt to understand that inspiration. We hope that Christianity points to God, shares in God, and participates in what God means, but God can never be limited to our Christian context. Until we accept this, our religious arrogance will violate his word against bearing false witness. Is it possible for us human beings, in the insecurity that marks our existence, to walk in the partial light of the truth that we can comprehend? Can we affirm that truth with deep conviction and power and at the same time remain aware that we always see through a glass darkly, we never see face to face?

We can acknowledge the possibility that every angle of vision will produce a new insight, and that the new insight is neither right nor wrong, it is just another way of comprehending. We can emotionally embrace the knowledge that God is like the sea beneath the sun—he always changes as we look out upon him, but in fact he never changes. It is our perception that is always changing.

Can we celebrate the truth that we do possess without using that truth to build up our sagging egos, to overcome our insecurity, to affirm our rightness, so that we must defend our truth or impose our truth? To follow Christ is a pilgrimage and an exploration that leads us into an unknown tomorrow where there are no landmarks and no certainties, where there is only the faith that God will be in every tomorrow if we but have the courage to enter it, to be open to it, to live in it, to be who we are without fear.

Christians are not settlers, but pilgrims. Whenever we become settlers, we put our wagons in a circle and we go to war. Christians are pioneers. The Christian life is always the life in process; it never arrives. Once you arrive with your Christian conviction, you become an idolator.

Christians are not keepers of museums who gather to admire the treasures of yesterday, though some of us act as if that is what we are. We are, rather, the bearers of the call of God to break every barrier, to expand every creed, every synthesis of yesterday, and to walk by faith into tomorrow, always searching and exploring and expecting a new revelation. Unless we know this, we will, out of our vast and all-consuming ignorance, inevitably and regularly violate the Commandment "You shall not bear false witness."

How very weary the holy God must get of our speaking of him in our shallow clichés! How weary he must get of our charges and countercharges as we seek to impose our limited vision upon him and defend it against one another! The only way to avoid the insidious and regular bearing of false witness is to escape the ignorance of being unaware of reality, the ignorance of being insensitive to the vastness of God's truth. As we grow older, we recognize that life begins to look different. We are wiser, we say. Not so, we are just older. Age does not give us wisdom; it just gives a new angle of vision. No better, no worse—just new. The fact is that we always think we are right from whatever angle of vision we look out upon life. We are always tempted to identify the reality that we perceive with the reality that is.

I can remember so well that as a young priest I would identify with the groom at every wedding. As I grew older, with daughters reaching toward those marriageable years, I suddenly realized I was looking at weddings through the eyes of the father of the bride, and the weddings looked very different. Marriages look different and feel different when you identify with a different participant. I still do not know, and probably never will, what it looks like to view a marriage through the eyes of the bride, or through the eyes of the mother of the bride or the mother of the groom.

There is nothing objective about your experience or mine. The minute we think there is, we violate the ninth Commandment. "You shall not bear false witness" is thus a call to escape the ignorance that plagues and distorts all human beings. "You shall not bear false witness" is a call to a new awareness, to a new sensitivity. It is a call to come out of the ignorance of our killing prejudices, the blindness of presuming that our view of life is objective, the slavery that comes with identifying our partial truth with the ultimate truth.

"You shall not bear false witness" is a call to a life that is open, free, vulnerable, and risky, but that is where life is lived, and that is where its meaning is found.

"Know thyself" is ancient wisdom. Know thy limitations. Know thy blindness. For only as we do does the need to bear false witness begin to fade, and the vicious, self-serving attacks of our human tongues upon the sacredness of life begin to cease.

13

Coveting–
The All-Embracing Word

According to the twentieth chapter of the Book of Exodus, the tenth Word of the Lord to the people of the Covenant has to do with the sin of coveting. That Commandment reads quite simply "You shall not covet." In a sense the Commandments have now run full circle, for this tenth Commandment is but a call to act out on the level of human behavior all of the implications of the first Commandment. "You shall not covet" is the behavioral application of "You shall have no other gods but me."

In many ways this Word on coveting is the most profound Word, the all-embracing Commandment; for it turns us away from the level of external deeds and it rivets our attention on the heart of the human being. This Commandment speaks to the deepest level of human motivation. I suspect that it was no accident that this Commandment was placed last, for that is the memorable position. For the same reason, the back cover of *Time* or *Newsweek* is the most important and expensive advertising space in the entire magazine. The cover and the back page are always the best remembered. So it is with the Commandments: the first and the last are the ones that everyone can recall.

I suspect that this Commandment, on a literal level, is also the most difficult to keep. The other Commandments deal with actions, and we might be able to refrain from the overt act of killing, committing adultery, or stealing, but this Commandment deals with the inner attitudes, and obviously it is far more difficult to prohibit attitudes than it is to prohibit actions. The other Commandments, at least until Jesus reinterpreted them in the Sermon on the Mount, focus on the external level of human life somewhat like a photograph. But Commandment number ten focuses, without any reinterpretation, on the internal level. It is like a penetrating X-ray of the human heart.

First the typical block to misunderstanding that shallow and insensitive minds seem always ready to resurrect and place upon the Scriptures must be removed. There is, in the minds of some people, a simplistic identification of the Commandment against coveting with an injunction against desire. I do not believe the text will support that identification. For if human desire is to be prohibited, so also will human growth, human progress, human stature, and wider human vision be prohibited.

The abolition of desire from the human spirit would produce a static life where human differences would not be allowed or noticed. Buddhism suggests that the way to peace is to kill the desire; but Christianity does not. Communism teaches that the way to peace is to make everything so equal that no one would have any reason to envy anyone else, and the perfect classless society would result, but Christianity does not concur in that assessment.

Desire is not wrong or evil. However the object of our ultimate desire will determine whether the desires of the human heart give us life or give us death. Both Buddhism and communism are systems which greatly diminish the human spirit. A just society will be built, I believe, on equality of opportunity, equality of education, equality of essence and value in every human being, equality of every child of God in the sight of God; but equality of being or equality of talents is not the human right to bestow, for it belongs to the God of creation alone. Part of the Creator's call to his creature is to rise to the maximum level of his or her potential, to be all that he or she is capable of being. For some that is more than for others. God's call to us is to be so at one with the self we are, so complete in our own being, so satisfied to accept ourselves as we are, that we do not envy or resent the self that someone else is. That is the Judeo-Christian vision of creation. Desire is a good part of life, when it is rightly understood. It is not evil.

In the public arena, I have always favored an absolutely free and open society, but I would resist the imposition of an egalitarian society. By this I mean that society should have within it all of the accoutrements of wealth and success. There *should* be exclusive neighborhoods, private schools for those who want them and can afford them. There should be private clubs where membership is conferred as a sign of success and of recognition. To me these things are important, for if they become desirable enough in the society as a whole, they serve to inspire creativity, industry, and hard work throughout the whole population in order to achieve these desirable goals.

My quarrel with the guardians of the establishment is not that these things are bad, but rather that the establishment leaders use artificial barriers, such as race and religion and ethnic origin, to exclude certain segments of the population from ever having the opportunity to enjoy these fruits of the good life. Consequently, some people are not allowed to enjoy the symbols of their own success. Everyone who achieves should be welcomed into those arenas where the symbols of success are enjoyed. Blacks and Jews should be eligible to live in any neighborhood or to be members of any club on the same basis as anyone else. I wish I believed that Christians across this nation were working to bring these things about.

My dream for America is not a dreary level of mediocrity where everyone is reduced to a common denominator. No, my dream for America is for an aristocracy based on achievement, rather than an aristocracy based on the accident of birth, or the color of skin, or whether you are a Wasp or a southern European in ancestry.

I see nothing wrong with honest ambition, drive, excellence, and hard work. Those who exhibit these qualities should be rewarded with all of the success symbols a society has to confer. However those qualities need to be employed for their own sake because they are good. They stretch the potential of every human being to do the best that he or she can with his or her talent. The qualities I have listed become destructive only when they are employed in order to defeat another person or to take something away from another rather than to stretch one's own being. The person who wants to do well enough to win is covetous. The person who acts so that all of his or her powers, talents, and gifts might be stretched to their limits is in the arena of what I would call legitimate desire.

There is a tremendous public responsibility that goes with creating a truly open and just society. The failure of the leaders of that society to take seriously that tremendous responsibility, or not to fulfill it adequately, literally invites the alienated people of the society to overturn it and impose an egalitarian principle upon it. Insensitive establishment people feed the desires that communism represents. The masses will not be exploited by any system forever. Exploitation always creates its own pay day, and the more the exploitation, the more violent that pay day is. If we could have seen the exploitation of the peasants in czarist Russia, we would have understood the frenzy of the Marxist revolution.

An open society must be truly open. History has taught us that everyone within the society must have an opportunity or it will become so fragile it will collapse in revolution. The barriers to openness have to be removed in order to preserve the society. The sources of exploitation have to be done away with, and there must be a commitment on the part of the society to right the wrongs of the past.

Vast public funds must be spent to overcome the inequities of opportunity. An open society must inject hope anew into every generation, no matter how hopeless the environment has been in the past. If I were running the government, I would see to it that school districts that serve the poor would have a larger share of the tax revenue than school districts that serve the affluent, for in the poor districts there is far more ground to be made up to provide the open equality of opportunity, and equality of opportunity must be a part of every just society.

I am convinced that tax structures need to be overhauled. The inequitable tax burden that falls on the poor and the middle class must be redressed; the loopholes available to the wealthy must be closed so that our society can be preserved. In an open society complete mobility based on ability alone can be accomplished. The citizenry might then be able to meet opportunity with real hope. The legitimate desire that resides in every person might be stretched to the limit of that person's capacity.

We must separate, with the sharp scalpel of theological clarity, the legitimate human desire from the human sickness that plagues our souls, the sickness called "covetousness." Desire is good. I applaud those people who are greedy for life, who seek its meaning openly and honestly, who are willing to taste its sweetness, who luxuriate in its beauty, experience its depths, and scale its heights. Life is the primary place in which the biblical God makes himself known. The full and even the infinite capacity of Jesus of Nazareth to be alive is one of the incontrovertible signs of his divinity, his oneness with God, his revelation of God in human history. His call, "I have come that you might have life and have it abundantly," is the essential call of the Christian Gospel. Christian ministry must open other lives to this transcendent dimension so that all of us are called to a new level and a new quality of being, a new meaning, a new capacity to live. I see the restlessness within us human beings, the sense of discontent with what we are and who we are, to be no less than the grip of God's grace upon us, echoing St. Augustine's cry in his *Confessions*: "Thou, o God, hast made us for thyself alone, and our hearts are restless until they find their rest in thee."

This is the level of legitimate desire, the seeking, the searching, the yearning for the ineffable and ultimately real, the holy God, a desire, a seeking, a searching, and a yearning that is not separate from our call to live fully, to love completely, to exist courageously. That is good.

Coveting is misplaced desire. Coveting is the act of placing a thing or the momentary fulfillment of a need into that ultimate place of worship and thus allowing that thing or that need fulfillment to color and distort our lives. Covetousness is, on the level of human behavior, the acting out of an idolatry. It is pretending that something other than God can finally give us life and make us full. It is the failure to see the fullness of God. It is not to comprehend the oneness, the holiness, the centrality of Yahweh, who is, for the Judeo-Christian tradition, the God of life, the ruler of history, the source of love, the ground of being, the height and depth of life. Covetousness is ignorance of the God who is over and under and around and through all that there is. Yet this God is wholly other, for this is the God we meet in the biblical drama. This is the God who is known and seen in creation, met in the Exodus, confronted at Mount Sinai—the God who now makes a Covenant with his people and speaks these Ten Words. This God we can desire legitimately, with an eternal restlessness that ever seeks and never fully finds. This desire always calls and drives us beyond ourselves, beyond contentment, beyond peace of mind, toward both the fullness of life and the fullness of God.

But when my desire fastens on anything less than God, it immediately becomes destructive, for that is where desire turns into covetousness, and covetousness will rob my life of its potential because it will narrow my vision, depress my limits, bring me to the edge of death, violate my purpose in creation, and starve my life to death. To covet is to fill the empty spaces of my God-directed desire with things. To covet is to believe that something less than God will satisfy the deepest human hunger in my heart. To covet is to think that something less than God will make me feel adequate or secure. To covet is to respond to things as if they somehow are ultimate or eternal or saving. To covet is to create idols, to be blasphemous. To covet is to be unaware that God is God. It is to be unaware of life's deepest meaning. It is to be insensitive to the gentle nudgings of the Spirit.

The proof of the destructiveness of coveting is that it is a disease that is not cured when the objects of one covetous desire are finally achieved, for to achieve a thing is never to satisfy the human heart. We only raise the ante. We yearn for more of the same, or we seek a new frontier that perhaps will fill us full, make us whole, and give us life and fulfillment. Unfortunately, things will never do that. All of this world's goods cannot fill the empty spaces of one human heart. All of this world's status, honor, and prestige cannot overcome the insecurity of one human life, for we all have deep within us that God-shaped hole, and nothing else will ever fit there. When we seek to fill that hole with anything less than God, we initiate a process of self-destruction.

The only cure for covetousness is prevention. If there is a

vacuum in our life where God ought to be, we will fill that vacuum with something; for the human heart, like nature itself, abhors a vacuum. To be in a Covenant relationship with the holy God is to know the infinite, precious quality of your self, and the infinite precious quality of everyone else's self. It is to be aware of the wholeness and the holiness of life. It is to allow the natural desire within us to call us into the fullness of life as people embraced by the love of God. That and that alone is what allows us to refrain from coveting.

"You shall not covet" thus concludes the holiest Ten Words of the Jewish Law. Purposefully, this is the final Word, for it is a summation of all the other Commandments. For when our life expresses the image of God and is in touch with the infinite, life-giving, self-fulfilling love of God, when God is the source and goal of our deepest desire, then and only then do we children of God live out creation's purpose. Only then do we know that god is one, and there can be no other gods than this.

In fulfilling the final Commandment, there would be no need to take the holy name of God in vain. Then, there would be no reason to violate the holy day when rest kindles the holy spark of God within us. We would honor the maleness and the femaleness of creation, aware that in this union is a sacrament of life itself and that in this vision is life-giving wholeness. We would do honor to all of life, preserving it, nurturing it, and letting it grow in every individual expression without being threatened and wanting to annihilate someone who hurts or who is different. We would honor personhood, expressed in the sacred bodies that we each possess, through which the self is manifested—the holy and precious self; for our wholeness would be such that we would never need to use another person in any relationship, whether it be physical, emotional, or spiritual. We could be free of the grasping quality that drives us to cheat and steal, to organize our world to our advantage and to another's disadvantage. We could be aware of our own subjectivity, our partial vision, our distorted ignorance that causes us to bear false witness.

So we come full circle. We discover that the tenth Commandment is but a reiteration of the first. It drives home the reality that God is God, that there is no other truth separate from that truth, and that that truth permeates every crack and crevice of life. These Ten Commandments illuminate every human emotion. They baptize every human relationship, and capture time. They invest time with a quality of timelessness, making every now a moment to share in eternity.

These Ten Words, these Ten Commandments, are thus as ancient as Sinai and, at the same time, as modern as tomorrow. Every generation must hear them, read, mark, learn, and inwardly digest them. Every generation must then interpret them anew in the light of the new occasions of the new day, for that is the eternal task of the people of the Covenant, whether it be the Old Covenant or the New Covenant, the Old Testament or the New Testament.

Jesus, our Christ himself, did this. A man went to him on one occasion, urging him to delineate which of the Commandments was the greatest. It was a kind of reductionist approach. "If I cannot keep them all, Lord, which one should I concentrate on?" is the burden of that question.

Jesus paused momentarily. Then he declined to respond to the specific content. "These Ten Words cannot be separated," he said in effect, "for they are but separate parts of an interlocking whole. They cannot be pitted against each other in some priority list. But they can be summarized," and this summary Jesus proceeded to give us.

"If you would keep the Commandments," he said, "you would love God with all of your heart, with all your mind, with all your strength, with all your being. And you would love your neighbor with the same love with which you love yourself. You are to love God; you are to love your neighbor; you are to love yourself. On these things hangs all of God's Law," Jesus said.

The Covenant people received the Law. Their narrative history portrays it as being first given at the foot of Mount Sinai some twelve hundred fifty years before the birth of Jesus. That Law and that Covenant are renewed every time a new life enters the life of the people of God.

The Ten Commandments are now complete, but the full body of the Jewish Law is still to come in all of its cultic detail.

That Law dominates the balance of the Book of Exodus. It covers every facet of human relationships; it spells out punishment for crime; it states the way children, servants, and animals are to be treated; it gives directions in intimate detail for worship, sacrifice, burnt offering, dressing the altar, and a thousand other details. It stretches past the Book of Exodus into Numbers, Leviticus, and Deuteronomy.

The remainder of the Book of Exodus has only a few narrative sections. On one of Moses' trips up the mountain, he stays too long with God, and the people ask Aaron to make them golden calves to worship. Aaron complies. Moses returns, and there is a vindictive moment of judgment. This is where Moses smashes the two tablets of stone on which, presumably, the Ten Commandments are written.

The Book of Exodus constantly builds Moses up. He alone speaks face to face with God. God's pillar of cloud rests upon Moses' tent each day. Moses returns to the mountain, and God rewrites the Ten Commandments on new stone, presumably to replace the previous ones that were broken. In this way, the later editors of the Torah harmonize the fact that there was more than one version of the Ten Commandments.

The Book of Exodus closes with the people of Israel busily engaged in building a proper sanctuary for the Lord. It is a portable sanctuary, for they are still a pilgrim people destined to wander for some forty years as nomads in the wilderness, learning, worshiping, preparing for the day when they claim the Land of the Promise and make it their holy land forever.

I hope that the message of the Bible once again is fresh and relevant to the complex life of our twentieth century. I hope that underneath its words, which are culturally conditioned words, filled with a vocabulary and with the concepts of a world that is no longer, the truth of God is revealed. The Bible is the Word of God, but the words of the Bible are not the words of God, and that is a crucial difference. The Word of God is still heard beneath the words of Scripture, and that Word of God still gives life wherever it is spoken. In the case of our Lord, who was the Word of God incarnate speaking to human history, that Word gives life wherever it is lived.

Hear the Word beneath the words, and enter the experience

of worship. Respond to the God of the Covenant not with pious activity but by living to the limit of your capability, by loving to the deepest capacity of your life, by being all that you are capable of being. It is in our commitment to live that we worship the God of life. It is in our commitment to love that we worship the God of love. It is in our commitment to be that we worship the God who is the infinite ground and ultimate source of all being. That is the call of God, the call of God's Word. That is the call of him who said, "I have come that you might have life and that you might have it abundantly."